TEACH US
TO FAST AND PRAY

"For Such a Time As This"

TEACH US TO FAST AND PRAY

"For Such a Time As This"

KIM JOHNSON

Teach Us to Fast and Pray:
For Such a Time as This

by Kim Johnson

© 2001, Word Aflame Press
Hazelwood, MO 63042-2299
Printing history: 2002, 2006

All Scripture quotations in this book are from the King James Version of the Bible unless otherwise identified.

Printed in the United States of America

WORD AFLAME PRESS
8855 Dunn Road, Hazelwood, MO 63042
www.pentecostalpublishing.com

Library of Congress Cataloging-in-Publication Data

Johnson, Kim
    Teach us to fast and pray : "for such a time as this" / by Kim Johnson.
        p. cm.
    ISBN 1-56722-560-8
    1. Fasting. 2. Prayer—Christianity. I. Title.

BV5055.J64 2001
248.4'7—dc21

                                                    2001026793

TABLE OF CONTENTS

Part Two

ACKNOWLEDGMENTS

This book is dedicated to the greatest intercessor I will ever know, Jesus Christ, and to all those who have influenced my life regarding prayer.

My life of prayer did not begin after obeying Acts 2:38; it began as a child. I distinctly remember both of my grandmothers, Margaret Koepke and Olive Johnson, spending countless hours teaching me how to pray the "Our Father" prayer. My parents, Roger and Georgia Johnson, also greatly influenced my prayer life with bedtime prayer, family devotions, and Sunday school. In addition, my Grandfather Johnson and Great-grandfather Wright gave their lives to prayer and to the Word of God. I wholeheartedly believe that the course of my life has been altered forever because of their prayers.

As a child, I learned to pray simple prayers. I also learned how to cry out to God when I was in trouble, which seemed to be quite often while growing up. Although I learned to pray at a young age, prayer was never a priority. It was not until I was born again into the kingdom of God that prayer became a lifestyle. It was then that I learned that prayer is not only taught, but also caught. If you surround yourself with people who pray, you cannot help but get involved with the spirit of prayer.

Before you are born again (John 3:3, 5; Acts 2:38), you can only pray from your own knowledge and understanding.

This makes the scope of prayer very limited. But after you receive the Spirit of God, God begins to pray through you, and prayer takes on a whole new dimension. It is from this dimension of prayer that one cultivates an intimate relationship with Jesus Christ.

If you have never obeyed Acts 2:38—repentance, baptism in the name of Jesus Christ for the remission of sins, and the infilling of the Holy Ghost (God's Spirit dwelling inside of you)—I encourage you to pray and ask God to direct you into this life-changing experience. It will enable you to walk with God in a dimension you have only heretofore dreamed about.

After I was born again, God surrounded my life with godly men and women who knew how to pray. I will always remember men and women, such as Reverend William Sciscoe, who baptized me and gave me my first prayer clock; Vesta Mangun, whose life and message *Power of Prevailing Prayer* influenced me to press into that deep place of prayer; Reverend Robert Mitchell, who told me that to be mightily used of God I needed to pray two to six hours every day; Reverend James Kilgore, whose family stories about prayer ignited a flame of desire for old fashioned prayer; Reverend and Mrs. Teklemariam Gehazagne, whose testimonies of answered prayer expanded my vision for revival through prayer; Thetus Tenney, who has unselfishly given of herself to whomever hungers for a deeper prayer life; Freddi Trammel, who has believed in me when I couldn't believe in myself; Reverend Nathaniel Haney, who taught me how to break strongholds through prayer; Reverend Lee Stoneking, whose example of prayer and Christian living has kept me focused on Calvary; Reverend Billy Cole, who taught me how to intercede with faith and balance; and Reverend T. W. Barnes, whose prayer life and wise counsel have directed me into the realm of unlimited possibilities with God.

In addition, God has surrounded my life with friends and acquaintances who love to pray. Without such a network of friends, my walk with God would not be what it is today. Thank you, friends.

A special thank you goes to Laurie Nelson, Frances Adams, and Wendy Danowski, who have unselfishly given of themselves to see God do something with my life, which includes the publishing of this book. Thank you for your example of sacrifice. It has so influenced my life to do all that I can do to see you and all those who dream of being used of God reach their potential in Jesus.

Also, a special thank you goes to Laura Bachman for her sacrifice and expertise in editing this book.

I want to thank my pastors, Frank Tamel and Anthony Tamel, and their beautiful wives and the saints of Parkway Apostolic Church. There is nothing more liberating to a saint of God than pastors who will release you to be all that you can be in the kingdom of God. There is nothing more empowering than a family of God that supports you and stands behind you through thick and thin. Thank you.

Finally, I want to thank my wonderful Savior, Jesus

Christ, for His endless mercy and grace, without which my prayer life would be in vain. I also want to thank Him for His example of continual intercession for all of us and for His immortal words: "My house shall be called of all nations the house of prayer" (Mark 11:17).

PREFACE

Oftentimes, fasting and prayer are taught as two separate spiritual disciplines that believers practice in order to develop their relationship with Jesus. Yet we find in the Bible that fasting and prayer go together like a hand and glove. Fasting and prayer humbles the soul enabling it to submit to the Spirit and to the purpose of God. And a soul that is submitted manifests the power and providence of God.

Prayer comes forth from our spirit. It is how we communicate with our Creator. Fasting deals with our outer man and brings cleansing to our inner man. When our undisciplined flesh rises up, oppression comes to our inner man. Flesh is so easy to puff up. It is like flour and water—all it needs is a little yeast to rise. And because we are subject to this world and have the knowledge of good and evil, we need to check constantly for leaven in our flesh (Galatians 5:9). Fasting aids in helping us to see what the Spirit of truth wants to reveal when He is searching our hearts for sin. Fasting humbles our human nature and opens up our spirit to hear from God. It also reveals to God the sincerity of our hearts. The sacrifices of God are a broken and contrite spirit (Psalm 51:17).

Fasting is presenting our bodies as a living sacrifice to God (Romans 12:1), and prayer then goes forth from a position of contrition and brokenness instead of pride and arrogance. It produces humility and a repentant heart by which God is able to turn and answer our prayers. It removes the blindness of pride so that we are able to fear God and to act appropriately in His presence.

Another aspect of prayer and fasting is its close association with the "word of faith" that we speak (Romans 10:8). Proverbs 18:21 says, *"Death and life are in the power of the tongue: and they that love it shall eat the fruit thereof."* Jesus Himself conveyed this powerful principle when He expounded on faith and speech: *"Have faith in God. For verily I say unto you, That whosoever shall say unto this mountain, Be thou removed, and be thou cast into the sea; and shall not doubt in his heart, but shall believe that those things which he saith shall come to pass; he shall have whatsoever he saith. Therefore I say unto you, What things soever ye desire, when ye pray, believe that ye receive them, and ye shall have them"* (Mark 11:22-24).

Jesus said that His words are spirit and life (John 6:63). He also said, *"And I speak to the world those things which I have heard of him. . . . When ye have lifted up the Son of man, then shall ye know that I am he, and that I do nothing of myself; but as my Father hath taught me, I speak these things"* (John 8:26, 28). Therefore, we conclude that if we speak forth the Word of God in faith believing we speak forth life. On the other hand if we speak forth words rooted in evil, negativity, doubt, and unbelief, we speak forth death. This principle of speech is fundamental in developing our relationship with God and understanding the relationship between fasting and prayer.

So what do our words have to do with prayer and fasting? First of all, let's examine the power of words. Israel wandered forty years in the wilderness because of their words. Samson's words ensnared him. God upheld Samuel's words all the days of his life—not one fell to the ground. Daniel received an angelic visitation because of his words. God told Hosea the prophet to *"take with you words, and turn to the LORD: say unto him, Take away all iniquity, and receive us graciously: so will we render the calves of our lips"* (Hosea 14:2). Jesus fasted forty days and nights to overcome the devil with His words.

Words are the vehicle that creates a life's past, present, and future. The tongue's function is to reveal the hidden self: one's thoughts, ideas, and personality. The tongue takes these hidden elements from within the person and through words brings them out into the open. A person's logic and reasoning are made manifest by his words. His ambitions and desires are penned in the heavens with his words. Jesus said, *"By thy words thou shalt be justified, and by thy words thou shalt be condemned"* (Matthew 12:37). The ultimate judge of all mankind will be the Word of God—and yet man continues to rush headlong into an inferno of misery because he does not recognize the corrupt and puffed up nature that fuels his speech.

The disciples of Jesus could not cast out a devil with their words because their hearts were full of doubt and unbelief. It wasn't that they didn't try, but when they tried, they were unsuccessful. Jesus told them that they lacked faith and that they could only cultivate powerful faith through fasting and prayer (Mark 9:29). Why only by fasting and prayer? Could it be that fasting and prayer enable us to speak forth the word of faith? Matthew 8:16 says, *"When the even was come, they brought unto him [Jesus] many that were possessed with devils: and he cast out the spirits **with his word**, and healed all that were sick."*

In the Old Testament, it was the faith of men and women that caused them to seek God's ways through fasting and prayer. (See Hebrews 11.) Their actions moved God to manifest His grace in their lives. Oftentimes, we read about those who made supplications to God through fasting and prayer. The word *supplication* in Hebrew is the same word for *grace*. Hence, the Old Testament patriarchs knew how to access the favor of God through fasting and prayer.

There are many other examples in the Bible of those who accessed God's favor through fasting and prayer. For example, Nehemiah, the cupbearer of King Artaxerxes, received words that brought anguish to his soul. In response, Nehemiah sought God by way of fasting and prayer, and God intervened mightily to destroy the works of the enemy against Nehemiah.

In the Book of Acts, we read about a devout Gentile named Cornelius who feared God and prayed always. Cornelius said, *"Four days ago I was fasting until this hour; and at the ninth hour I prayed in my house, and, behold, a man stood before me in bright clothing"* (Acts 10:30). Cornelius was a man who had learned the art of fasting and prayer. Fasting and prayer prepared Cornelius to receive a messenger from God, divine instruction, and salvation for his entire house.

Daniel's fasting and prayer life was the mark of his success with God and man. Daniel 9:3 says, *"And I set my face unto the LORD God, to seek by prayer and supplications, with fasting, and sackcloth, and ashes."* Daniel used fasting and prayer to seek God's favor and understanding for himself and the captive nation of Israel. The humility of fasting coupled with repentance moved the heart of God to bestow on Daniel the ability to understand the visions that God had given him pertaining to Israel's future. In Daniel 10, we again read of Daniel humbling himself through fasting. Daniel 10:12 states that Daniel's words were heard in heaven from the first day he set his heart to understand and to chasten himself before God. The result was that God sent an angel to Daniel because of Daniel's words. Notice that Daniel set his heart to seek and to understand God. He obtained the desire of his heart through fasting, which God called *chastening*. The Hebrew word for *chasten* in this passage is *anah*. This word means "to abase self, afflict, answer, chasten self, deal hardly with, defile, exercise, force, humble self, hurt, ravish, submit self, weaken." God heard and responded to Daniel because Daniel was willing to humble himself before God and to depend on God alone for help. God always responds to those who are humble before Him. Jesus said, *"Blessed are the poor in spirit: for theirs is the kingdom of heaven"* (Matthew 5:3). The word *poor* in this passage is from the Greek *ptochos*, meaning "beggar (-ly), poor."

I remember a time while I was on a fast that there were

some accusations made against my character. I took the accusations before God and asked Him to search me to see if there was any truth to these words. The Lord then began to reveal a pattern in my life that was contrary to His Word and ways. Hence, I was able to repent of this pattern, thus enabling God to deliver me from my sin. Fasting done properly with the proper motives moves the heart of God.

Another example of how fasting and prayer work together is King David's intercession for his newborn son. When King David's newborn son became sick, following God's judgment for David's sin, David fasted for his son until the child died. King David understood the mercy of God. He knew that by humbling himself before God there was a possibility that God would turn back judgment and heal his son. Although God did not change His mind, God did honor David's humility and brokenness of heart by rewarding him with another child, Solomon.

Isaiah 58, which is discussed extensively in the fasting portion of this book, shows how fasting is more than just afflicting the flesh; it is drawing out the soul, i.e., moving from selfishness to selflessness. God said the purpose of fasting was not to make your voice heard on high but to humble yourself and to draw yourself out to others. The results will draw His mercy and grace near, and He will hear and answer your prayers. It is similar to the fast of Esther: her voice was not heard during the fasting, but the fast itself gained her favor with God and King Ahasuerus, causing her petition to be heard. Fasting puts us in a position to approach God for our petition and to hear God's answer.

Paul taught believers to crucify their flesh so that they might walk in the Spirit. Walking in the Spirit is more than being led by the Spirit in action; it is also speaking and praying according to the will of the Spirit. Therefore, fasting puts us in a position to rid ourselves of fleshly mindsets and yokes that cause us to pray and to speak contrary to the Word and will of God. Jesus said, *"If you abide in me, and my words abide in you, ye shall ask what ye will, and it shall be done unto you"* (John 15:7).

May we learn to walk as our spiritual forefathers did: humbly and prayerfully before God. May our lives of fasting, coupled with prayer, move us to the place that enables us to speak the word of faith and to see God manifest His power in and through our lives.

Part One

FASTING

Author's Note

Fasting has been a part of God's plan through the ages. Oftentimes when we think about fasting, all we think about is the self-denial (lack of food) or the hunger we are going to have to endure through a fast. Although denial is part of the fast, it is not the purpose of the fast.

Fasting coupled with prayer has brought answers, direction, and protection from God through the ages. What is God's purpose for fasting? What did fasting accomplish in the lives of our spiritual forefathers? Why is fasting so necessary today? How do we fast unto the Lord? When does God call us to fast? Who is called to fast? How does fasting affect our health? How often should we fast? These questions and more will be answered as we embark on this study of biblical fasting.

Chapter One

WHAT IS FASTING?

The verb *fast* in the Hebrew is *tsuwm*. It literally means "to cover the mouth." The *American Heritage Dictionary* defines the verb *fast* as "to abstain from food; to eat very little or abstain from certain foods, especially as a religious discipline." The noun *fast* is defined as "the act or practice of abstaining from or eating very little food. A period of such abstention or self-denial." Biblical fasting is more than covering the mouth and abstaining from all or certain foods to achieve personal gain. Biblical fasting is always accompanied with a burden, i.e., a desperate desire and purpose that necessitates drawing close to God. Fasting without a burden and a purpose just weakens the flesh. A burden is the key to successful fasting in the kingdom of God. Love for God and love for one's neighbor is what produces a burden. It is the underlying purpose and motive that drives one to fast. It is a burden for the lost that will compel one to fast for them. It is a burden to see deliverance and healing in someone's life that will cause one to fast for that person's deliverance and healing. It is a burden to subdue the kingdom of darkness and to usher in the kingdom of heaven that will cause one to fast. It is a burden to know Jesus and to conquer the flesh that will drive one to fast. A burden coupled with desire and fasting coupled with repentant prayer move the heart of God to favor us. *Fasting simply out of religious duty will never change the heart of God in our situation.*

Jesus is looking for those who are willing to humble their hearts and to bring themselves under the yoke of His cross, so that He can impart His burden for the lost to them. We can draw a comparison between Simon of Cyrene being commanded to carry the Lord's cross to Calvary, i.e., to carry the Lord's burden, and our bearing the Lord's burden for sinners for whom He died. Jesus knew that after His ascension He would be able to impart His burden to millions through the outpouring of His Spirit (Acts 1:8). Therefore, let us prepare ourselves through fasting to take up His burden and to follow Him.

It is my prayer that the eyes of our understanding will always be opened to see the blessings and benefits of fasting unto the Lord. May fasting no longer be a drudgery or duty but an avenue by which we come to see the power of God manifested in our lives, homes, jobs, and cities.

Chapter Two

ISAIAH 58:
GOD'S CHOSEN FAST

In Isaiah 58, God reveals His chosen fast. He grants us understanding concerning His plan, His purpose, and His rewards for fasting. Let us look at God's call for Israel to fast.

Isaiah 58:1

Isaiah 58 begins with a commandment from God to the prophet Isaiah: *"Cry aloud, spare not, lift up thy voice like a trumpet, and shew my people their transgression, and the house of Jacob their sins."* This statement reveals the urgency with which God wanted to speak to His people. He foresaw the coming destruction and annihilation of his people because of their sins and transgressions, and He no longer could remain silent.

Why was Isaiah to lift up his voice like a trumpet? The trumpet (Hebrew, *shofar*) is an instrument that produces a very strong, clear sound that can be heard from afar. In Bible days, it was used to awaken the people and to get their attention—to gather them for war as well as for instruction.

The Lord wanted Isaiah's speech to be clear and strong so that there would be no misunderstanding what God was saying to His people. The cry was to be from the heart of God, a *burden* not only heard but piercingly felt. He wanted Isaiah to speak with authority and purpose so that (1) the people would know they were hearing from God and (2) that they would have no excuse when judgment was executed.

Isaiah 58:2-5

The Lord then proceeded to tell Isaiah the problem. The problem was that the people of Israel sought God like a nation that actually knew Him, when in reality they did not. They were idolatrous and blinded by their own self-righteousness and pride. They approached His throne haughtily instead of humbly. They acted as if they were perfect, sinless, and upright before God. They could not, however, fool the all-knowing God of heaven and earth. He knew they were committing sins and transgressions that openly disgraced His name in the sight of other nations. When they fasted, they afflicted their flesh, but their hearts were not changed. *They wanted to be seen and heard, but they did not want to hear from God.* They fasted to accomplish their desire and purpose. This caused strife and debate among them, and a house divided cannot stand. What God was communicating to the people was that though they looked and acted the part, their hearts in reality were not toward Him or with Him. Moreover, they were stuck on themselves, and they had become blind to their own sins and transgressions.

Jesus spoke similar words to the Laodicean church in Revelation 3:17: *"Because thou sayest, I am rich, and increased with goods, and have need of nothing; and knowest not that thou art wretched, and miserable, and poor, and blind, and naked."* Here again, God lets us see the situation through His eyes. What men thought was religious and pleasing to God, Jesus said was wretched. Repeatedly, the Lord taught that He is not impressed with our materialism and riches in this world. What moves God is a heart that desires to know Him and to understand His ways. Jeremiah 9:23-24 reads, *"Thus saith the LORD, Let not the wise man glory in his wisdom, neither let the mighty man glory in his might, let not the rich man glory in his riches: but let him that glorieth glory in this, that he understandeth and knoweth me, that I am the LORD which exercise lovingkindness, judgment, and righteousness, in the earth: for in these things I delight, saith the LORD."* (See also Isaiah 43:10; Micah 6:8; John 17:3.)

Proverbs 21:2 says, *"Every way of a man is right in his own eyes: but the LORD pondereth the hearts."* We must have the right motive when fasting. To check your motive, begin your fast with a time of repentance. Pray Psalm 51 and ask God to cleanse you of any secret faults and wrong motives. Ask the Lord to establish a pure motive in your heart. Then entreat the Lord for His grace to fast and for a humble heart to hear His voice.

Isaiah 58:6-14

The Lord then went on to tell Isaiah the solution. The following is my paraphrase of vv. 6-14: "Listen, Israel! You're not going to fast the way you used to. You're going to fast the way that I tell you to. I'm going to choose the fast, and the fast that I choose is going to set you free from your sins and transgressions—not only you, but whomever you desire to see set free. It will not be a self-centered fast but a God-centered fast. It will not be a fast in which you make your voice heard on high. It will be a fast that causes *My* voice to be heard in your heart. The fast that I have chosen is a fast that enables you to be transparent with your family. You no longer will have to hide your iniquities or true character behind a mask or facade. You will be delivered. It is a fast that will cause you to reach out to others. It is a fast that will bring restoration between us. It will cause My glory to rest on you and My righteousness to guide you. It will cause you to be a repairer of breaches and a restorer of paths on which to walk. Above all, it will produce the thing I desire most: a people whose delight is in the Lord, a people who are the head and not the tail. A people who usher in My glory for all nations to behold!"

The lists below highlight Isaiah 58 from the *Tanakh* (A modern Jewish translation of the Hebrew Scriptures):

The Lord said *if you will:*
- remove perversion from your midst [and]
- finger pointing (accusations) [and]

- evil speech (vain and worldly speech) [and]
- offer your soul to the hungry and
- satisfy the afflicted (poor, suffering) soul

Then *I will* cause your:
- light to burst out like the dawn
- healing to speedily sprout, and
- righteous deeds to precede you

And *I will:*
- cause the glory of the Lord to gather you in
- respond to your cry and say, "Here I am!"
- guide you always
- satisfy your soul in times of drought, and
- strengthen your bones

And *you will:*
- be like a watered garden and a spring of water whose waters never fail
- rebuild ancient ruins
- restore generations-old foundations
- be called, "repairer of the breach," and
- "restorer of paths for habitation"

In conclusion, God's chosen fast is a sin-buster. I Peter 4:1-2 says, *"Forasmuch then as Christ hath suffered for us in the flesh, arm yourselves likewise with the same mind: for he that hath suffered in the flesh hath ceased from sin; that he no longer should live the rest of his time in the flesh to the lusts of men, but to the will of God."*

    There are many forms of suffering that the Lord can allow in our lives to help conform us to His will. Suffering is a part of our Christian walk. It aids in the development of humility, obedience, and righteousness in our lives. Fasting is a type of suffering that will humble our souls before God. King David said, "I humbled my soul with fasting" (Psalm 35:13). God will not overlook a contrite spirit and a humble heart. He will hear and answer the prayers of such a person. It is through the humbling of our souls and the entreating of God's delivering power that we are set free from carnal habits that cause us to sin. It is His anointing that breaks every yoke! When we humble ourselves, the Lord lifts us up!

Chapter Three

HOW TO FAST

Preparation

One of the best ways to prepare (submit) your flesh for a lifestyle of fasting is to meditate on and study scriptures pertaining to fasting. It is also good to adjust your diet to a healthier style of eating (this is discussed further in this book). The following is a word study on Isaiah 58:6. The definitions were obtained by using a common dictionary and a *Strong's Concordance*. (If you are unfamiliar with using a concordance, you can read the preface of the concordance for an explanation on how to use the book's features.) Word studies help us to grow in understanding and a deeper knowledge of the Scriptures. *Understanding is one of the greatest treasures we can receive from heaven.*

Proverbs 3:13 says, *"Happy is the man that findeth wisdom, and the man that getteth understanding."* Proverbs 4:7 states, *"Wisdom is the principal thing; therefore get wisdom: and with all thy getting get understanding."* Proverbs 9:6 says, *"Forsake the foolish, and live; and go in the way of understanding."* Jesus said, *"When any one heareth the word of the kingdom, and understandeth it not, then cometh the wicked one, and catcheth away that which was sown in his heart. This is he which received seed by the way side. . . . But he that received seed into the good ground [prepared heart] is he that heareth the word, and understandeth it; which also beareth fruit, and bringeth forth, some an hundredfold, some sixty, some thirty"* (Matthew 13:19, 23).

A Word Study

*"Is not this the fast that I have **chosen**? to loose the **bands of wickedness**, to **undo the heavy burdens** [bundles of yokes], and to **let the oppressed go free**, and that ye **break every yoke**?"* (Isaiah 58:6)

What does it mean to loose the bands of wickedness, undo the heavy burdens, let the oppressed go free, and break every yoke? In this word study, we will examine the words highlighted above to answer these questions.

Chosen

The word *chosen* means "to try, or select." It is a type of fasting God has selected. *Chosen* also means "favored by God."

Bands of Wickedness

A *band* means "a fetter (a shackle or chain for the feet, any type of restraint); a pain." It is also "a thin strip [not very visible] of wood, metal, rubber, etc., fastened around something to bind or tie it together." The word *bands* in

Hebrew comes from two words: *chariyts* and *charats*. *Chariyts* (char-eets) means "to slice or cut; hence a threshing-sledge (with sharp teeth)." *Charats* (char-ats) means "to point sharply, to wound." So, a band is an instrument or fastener that wounds.

Wickedness is "the quality or condition of being wicked as in a wicked action." In Hebrew, the word for *wickedness* is *rehshah* (ray-shah), and it means "a wrong (especially moral): iniquity." It comes from the word *rawshah* (raw-shah), which means "to be, do, or declare wrong; to disturb or violate. To vex, condemn, make trouble."

The word *wicked* is akin to *wicca,* which means "witch." *Wicked* is "having or resulting from bad moral character, evil, depraved." It is generally bad, painful, but without any moral consideration involved.

In summary, to loose the bands of wickedness means "to be loosed from a bad or perverse moral character (for example: sexual immorality, diverse lusts, pornography, homosexuality, smoking, drinking, lying, covetousness, gluttony, etc.)." It means "to be set free from afflictions and injustices caused by wickedness." Fasting also can destroy spiritual wickedness operating in high places (Ephesians 6:12).

The story of Esther opens our understanding to the power that fasting has to loose the bands of wickedness. Mordecai, Esther, her maidens, and the Jews of Shushan fasted three days. At the end of the third day, Esther put on her royal garments and went before the king. The king raised his royal scepter, granting her permission to draw near and to make her petition, which could include anything up to one-half of the kingdom. God also gave Esther divine wisdom for the purpose of overcoming an evil plot executed against her people (the Jews). Hence, Esther revealed the plot of the evil one, Haman, to the king, who in turn ordered Haman to be killed. This resulted in salvation for the Jews, not only in Shushan but throughout all the provinces under the king's rule.

Job 11:13-19 gives us further insight into the rewards obtained through loosing the bands of wickedness in our lives: *"If thou prepare thine heart, and stretch out thine hands toward him; if iniquity be in thine hand, put it far away [fast and repent], and let not wickedness dwell in thy tabernacle. For then shalt thou lift up thy face without spot; yea, thou shalt be steadfast, and shalt not fear: because thou shalt forget thy misery, and remember it as waters that pass away: and thine age [life with God] shall be clearer than the noonday; thou shalt shine forth, thou shalt be as the morning. And thou shalt be secure, because there is hope; yea, thou shalt dig about thee, and thou shalt take thy rest in safety. Also thou shalt lie down, and none shall make thee afraid; yea, many shall make suit unto thee."*

Undo the Heavy Burdens

Undo is a strong action word. It means "to open, release, or untie." It also means "to reverse the doing of, to do away with, to cancel, to put an end to, or to solve." In Hebrew, the word *nathar* (nahth-are) means "to jump, to be violently agitated; to terrify, to shake off, untie."

Heavy comes from the Hebrew word *mowtah* (mow-tah), which means "a yoke [something you can't get free from]." *Mowtah* comes from another word *mowt* (moat), which means "to waver; to slip, shake, fall."

In Hebrew the word *burden* is *aguddah* (agood-dah). It means "a bundle, a band, to bind, knot, a bunch, burden, or troop."

Let the Oppressed Go Free

To let and *go* mean "to send away, to send for, or to send out." The Hebrew word for *let* and *go* is *shalach* (shawl-ach).

Oppressed in the Hebrew is *ratsats* (rahtz-ahts), and it means "to crack in pieces, literally or figuratively; to break, bruise, crush, discourage, oppress, struggle together." The dictionary definition is "to press against; to weigh heavily on the mind, spirits, or senses of; to lie heavily on; burden; to keep down by cruel or unjust use of power or authority; to burden with harsh, rigorous impositions; to tyrannize over; to crush or trample down."

Free is *chophshy* (cough-shee) in Hebrew. It means "to be exempt from bondage, tax, or care: to have liberty; to spread loose [like eagles wings—to soar, fly]." It also means "to let go from the hand, to free from slavery."

Fasting can cause those who have been crushed in pieces, bruised, broken, discouraged, and/or oppressed to be set free. They can be delivered from their oppression and live in liberty. Jesus came to set the captives free (Luke 4:18). Isaiah 61:1 says, *"He hath sent me to bind up the brokenhearted, to proclaim liberty to the captives, and the opening of the prison to them that are bound."* Acts 10:38 says, *"How God anointed Jesus of Nazareth with the Holy Ghost and with power: who went about doing good, and healing all that were oppressed of the devil; for God was with him."* Jesus heals the oppressed, and the best way to access His healing is by faith in the power of His blood and the stripes He received for our healing. Fasting aids in enabling us to exercise our faith.

Break Every Yoke

The word *break* in Hebrew is *nathaq* (nahth-ahk). It means "to tear off: to break off, burst, draw away, lift up, pluck off, pull (out), root out." *Yoke* is the same word for *heavy* (Hebrew, *mowtah*). Again it means "an ox-bow; a yoke: bands, heavy, staves, yoke." *To break every yoke* means "to root out, tear off, pluck off, pull out, and burst every form of bondage [physical or mental]."

Breaking the Big Yoke: Food

God saved Israel for His name's sake that He might make His mighty power to be known. He showed them great and majestic signs and wonders. He delivered them from slavery and from all of their enemies; however, Psalm 106:13 says, *"They soon forgat his works; they waited not for his counsel."* Why? Verse 14 says, *"But lusted exceedingly in the wilderness, and tempted God in the desert."* All they could think about was the flesh pots (stew), leeks, and onions back in Egypt. Verse 15 further says, *"And he gave them their request;*

but sent leanness into their soul."

Almost every complaint Israel made to Moses had to do with food. They were always complaining: "We're thirsty, we're hungry, and we want meat now! We want to go back to Egypt so we can eat and drink from the pots of bondage instead of the promised wells of living water."

Jesus said it this way, *"Therefore I say unto you, Take no thought for your life, what ye shall eat, or what ye shall drink; nor yet for your body, what ye shall put on. Is not the life more than meat, and the body more than raiment? . . . For after all these things do the Gentiles seek:) for your heavenly Father knoweth that ye have need of all these things. But seek ye first the kingdom of God, and his righteousness; and all these things shall be added unto you"* (Matthew 6:25, 32-33).

During the days of Jesus, food was a major concern for His disciples. In John 4:4-35, we read about Jesus witnessing to a woman of Samaria. Here Jesus was right in the middle of a great revival in Samaria, and His disciples said, *"Master, eat."* Jesus turned to His disciples and said, *"I have meat to eat that ye know not of."* Shocked and a little taken aback, they said to one another, *"Hath any man brought him ought to eat?"* Jesus couldn't help but overhear and said, *"My meat is to do the will of him that sent me, and to finish his work. Say not ye, There are yet four months, and then cometh harvest? behold, I say unto you, Lift up your eyes [get your eyes off the food], and look on the fields; for they are white already to harvest."*

Matthew 24:38 says, *"For as in the days that were before the flood they were eating and drinking."* And Philippians 3:18-19 says, *"For many walk, of whom I have told you often, and now tell you even weeping, that they are the enemies of the cross of Christ: whose end is destruction, whose God is their belly, and whose glory is in their shame, who mind earthly things.*" Although we rarely consider our belly as a god, it is quite evident that it has the potential to be one. In America, as well as many other countries, people are enslaved to food. Our preoccupation with food can almost be pictured as an offering or sacrifice brought to appease a false god. How often do we respond to food advertisements or TV commercials by grabbing a quick bite to eat? Have you ever stopped a strong desire to pray by eating?

The Cross crucifies the lusts and affections of our flesh and opens the veil to the spirit world. When Jesus was on the cross, the world tempted Him to come down. The world is still tempting those who are crucified with Christ to come off the cross. The words of the apostle John still echo from afar: *"Love not the world, neither the things that are in the world. If any man love the world, the love of the Father is not in him. For all that is in the world, the lust of the flesh, and the lust of the eyes, and the pride of life, is not of the Father, but is of the world"* (I John 2:15-16).

When does eating cross the line between being acceptable in the eyes of God to being sin in the eyes of God? The answer lies in what is discussed above. Eating, in and of itself, is not sin, but the preoccupation with food and eating to excess is sin. Remember, our bodies are holy temples that house the Spirit of God. Eating has its place, which is secondary to the King's business. It is not always easy to put the Lord first when food is involved because we are so conditioned in our eating habits. We are trained to eat three meals a day from the time we are weaned—even when we are not hungry. What did Jesus say? *"Man shall not live by bread alone, but by every word that proceedeth out of the mouth of God"* (Matthew 5:4). Fasting helps us to break our life-long patterns of eating. We are also taught that eating is the source of our strength. But as Christians, the opposite is true. The Lord is our strength and shield! It is amazing how little food the body needs to maintain physical strength.

Fasting delivers us from the bondage of food. It causes us to *"lift up our eyes"* and to refocus the priorities of this life from the natural to the spiritual. We not only need to fast from food, but we also need to fast from things that stimulate our appetites such as television, advertisements, fast-food restaurants, desserts, food magazines, etc. It is time to help one another lift up our eyes to the harvest, for the fields are ripe (John 4:35)!

Chapter Four

THREE DIMENSIONS OF FASTING

E very fast mentioned in the Bible had a burden and a purpose behind it. The burden and purpose are more important to God than the actual act of fasting. There are predominantly three dimensions of fasting in the Bible. The order in which these dimensions are discussed does not depict their level of importance. They are only different aspects of fasting. All believers have the potential to practice these different dimensions of fasting in their lives.

The First Dimension: The Predetermined Fast

The *predetermined fast* is a fast in which the individual determines the purpose, length, and type of fast he or she is going to undertake. This type of fasting is practiced in virtually every culture. A predetermined fast is very helpful in disciplining our flesh and bringing it under subjection to the Spirit of God. *It is important to set aside at least one day a week for this type of fasting.* This discipline will help us establish a lifestyle of fasting. If you fast at least one day a week,

at the end of a year you will have fasted for fifty-two days.
You will have tithed more than ten percent of your days to
God. God will not overlook men and women who are will-
ing to commit themselves to this extent for His glory.
Consistency in fasting helps to prepare us for greater
things in God's kingdom.

The following guidelines can help you determine your
purpose and the length of your fast. These are just guidelines. You may need to develop your own guidelines as you
experiment with different lengths and disciplines of fasting:

- One-to-three-day fasts aid in subduing fleshly problems and desires, bringing favor, protection, salvation, and healing. (See Ezra 8:21-31; Esther 4:13-
  8:11; Acts 9:8-22; Colossians 3:5.)

- Three-to-ten-day fasts aid in breaking yokes in our
  families, receiving wisdom and understanding. (See
  II Samuel 12:16-17; Esther 4:13-8:11.)

- Ten-to-twenty-one-day fasts aid in breaking bands of
  wickedness and yokes over cities and nations. They
  bring direction and deliverance, revelation and understanding. (See Daniel 1:8-20; 10:2-12:13; Acts
  27:9-44.)

When fasting for long periods of time, it is prudent to
let a spiritual authority or mentor in your life know your

intentions. This individual will be able to pray for you and help you through any unforeseen physical or spiritual difficulties.

Are there times when we should break our fast? Yes. There are times when our fasting can be a stumbling block to others. The apostle Paul said, when you are bidden to eat, eat whatever is placed in front of you (I Corinthians 10:27). He went on to say, *"That no man put a stumbling block or an occasion to fall in his brother's way"* (Romans 14:13). Our decision to break or continue a fast must be ruled by the law of love, discernment, and discretion. For example, I was in the middle of a long fast, and my neighbor's wedding was approaching. I had made a commitment to attend the ceremony and reception several months before the fast. I thought about calling my neighbor and either not attending or requesting soup, but the Holy Ghost impressed me to go and eat. I attended the reception dinner and ate a delicious meal. My fast continued on schedule the next day. There were no physical ramifications, nor did my hunger return. God took care of every detail.

The Second Dimension: A God-Determined Fast

The second dimension of fasting is what I call a *God-determined (or Spirit-led) fast.* A God-determined fast consists of a time period when the Spirit of God leads us into fasting to hear from God. It is a consecrated fast accompanied by an intense burden to hear from God. You may or may not know the specific purpose. The Spirit's guidance will determine the length of a God-determined fast. He may impress on your heart a certain number of days to fast, or He may not. The fast ends when there is a release of God's burden and/or the return of hunger.

Moses, Elijah, Ezekiel, and Jesus all participated in God-determined fasts. These fasts were chosen by God to impart knowledge and anointing that would give direction to and determine the destiny of the people of God. Moses received the law and the Tabernacle plan. Elijah heard the still small voice of God and received instruction to go and anoint Hazael, Jehu, and Elisha. He was also given a word of knowledge regarding the prophets God had preserved. Ezekiel received the plans for the third Temple. Jesus overcame Satan and received instruction and an anointing that changed the world!

A God-determined fast should never be entered into lightly. It is to be a consecrated and holy period of time. During this type of fast, you will sense a strong desire to remove yourself from the fellowship of others and to spend your time with the Lord. It involves a time period when everything on your calendar is put on hold, except for those things the Lord gives you permission to do. This type of fasting is only for a season. When the Lord has spoken and His purpose is accomplished, He will lift the burden to fast. Your hunger will return, and you will resume daily life accordingly. It is good to keep a journal during the fast. This is a time when God will speak to you regarding specific matters pertaining to His will and His kingdom. This may include revelations and insight into future events.

Timing

Much of what the Lord may share with you should be kept in the heart until the appropriate time to be shared. It is important to pray for wisdom that enables us to know timing and judgment in every situation. This is often when we get into trouble. We want to share or implement everything right away. By doing this, we can be revealing secrets and treasures to the enemy without even knowing it. When something is spoken outside of God's timing, your words can give the devil insight that can greatly hinder what God has planned. Frequently, Satan and our flesh will fight us with doubt, unbelief, and fear after we have spoken words before their time. Everything has a season, and we need to learn how to distinguish seasons according to the plan of God in our lives.

In the past, you may have felt God leading you into a God-determined fast, but you were afraid. You may have been afraid of what others might say or think if you let go of your busy schedule to spend time with the Lord. You may also have had an intimidating experience from someone who did not feel that this type of fast was necessary. It is important not to overrule what God is leading you to do because of others. Too often the fear of rejection rules the lives of God's people instead of His will. This is a good time to overcome such fear and enter into the fear of God. God always prepares the way to do what He asks. Just gracefully bow out of your plans and enter into God's plans for that season. *If you will take care of God's business, He will always take care of yours.* I am amazed at how God intervenes and changes my schedule when I enter into a God-determined fast. If you feel God is leading you into this type of fast but have some doubts, talk to your spiritual authority, obtain counsel, and proceed accordingly.

The Third Dimension: Fasting Until

Herein lies the secret of receiving answers from God: waiting. *Fasting until* is a fast in which we entreat and seek the face of the Lord *until* the answer comes. It is a humbling of our souls and a waiting upon the Lord until. When a person approaches God to fast until, he is placing his situation wholeheartedly into God's hands. He is laying aside every preconceived notion, selfish desire, and personal motive. He is waiting to hear directly from God. He is trusting solely in God for his answer and not in man. We see this type of fast repeatedly in the Bible. King David fasted until he heard whether his son was going to live or die. Although his son's life was taken, God was so moved by the sacrifice and compassion King David displayed that He granted him another son by Bathsheba: Solomon (the next king of Israel). Daniel sought the Lord until he received understanding of the ages. In the Book of Acts, Cornelius fasted until salvation came to his household (Acts 10:30). The apostle Paul fasted until for the salvation of those he was sailing with (Acts 27:21-24).

Fasting until is a fast that is based on relationship, not works. When we fast until, two very important attributes are produced in our lives: patience and trust.

When you seek God to fast until, you need to determine whether or not you are going to eat any food, and if you do plan to eat, you must decide what types of food you will eat and when you will eat. If you eat during this time, it should be only for strength and not for pleasure. It is wise to pray and ask for the Lord's guidance to help determine your plan of action. When the Lord has impressed a plan upon your heart, you are less likely to detour from it. When you receive your answer from God, the fast is over. You then resume your daily living and do what God has told you to do.

Remember, the natural man came first, and the spiritual man second. When you are born again (John 3:3-5; Acts 2:38; Romans 6), you become a new person in Christ Jesus. All old things pass away. It is time for you to arise and claim your rightful inheritance of the treasures in God's kingdom. It is time for His Spirit to rule your life and your flesh. It's time for the manifestation of the children of God! Fasting quickens your awareness of the things of the Spirit and helps you take on the mind of Christ.

The Power of a Made-Up Mind

And thou, Solomon my son, know thou the God of thy father, and serve him with a perfect heart and with a willing mind.
1 CHRONICLES 28:9

In every decision a person makes, the human will is involved. When a person truly purposes in his heart and makes up his mind to do something, there is nothing that can deter him except death itself. The power that lies within our human wills "to be" or "not to be" is extraordinary. The human will plays a vital role in our successes and failures in the kingdom of God. The more we are willing to align our will (and our thoughts, emotions, and desires) with the Word of God and submit to His grace (enabling power and divine assistance), the greater our accomplishments will be.

Learn to lean upon God's grace to receive the will and determination you need to fast. Hebrews 4:16 says, *"Let us therefore come boldly unto the throne of grace, that we may obtain mercy, and find grace to help in time of need."* Fasting is not easy and can be physically challenging, to say the least. Therefore, you always benefit when you purpose in your heart to fast and completely submit your mind to the Spirit (meditating on the Word helps). In so doing, you will reach your goal.

One of the greatest battles you will ever fight in your walk with God is bringing your mind (will, thoughts, emotions, intellect) under subjection to the Spirit of God. Allowing the Spirit to rule your flesh and your mind comes through much breaking of the human will. Fasting aids in developing a humble mind and a poor (broken) spirit.

Chapter Five

THE BURDEN

The hour was late and quickly approaching midnight as Jesus led his disciples to the Garden of Gethsemane; the weight of eternity for billions of lost souls was descending on His heart. As they approached the garden and the burden became all-consuming, Jesus said to his disciples, *"My soul is exceeding sorrowful, even unto death: tarry ye here, and watch with me"* (Matthew 26:38). After separating Himself from His disciples, He collapsed under the weight of His coming ordeal. The burden for the eternal destiny of man since the fall of Adam consumed every fiber of His being. It was not facing death that brought Him to the garden; it was not the expectation of untold suffering that brought Him to the garden; it was the weight of the sins of the world that brought Him to the garden. It was a burden for your soul and my soul and the countless other souls of men and women before and after the incarnate life of Jesus that drove Him to the garden. He was making intercession for all transgressors. He was pouring out His soul unto death, even the death of the cross.

When Jesus prayed, *"O my Father, if it be possible, let this cup pass from me: nevertheless not as I will, but as thou wilt"* (Matthew 26:39). He was speaking on behalf of His people, who were appointed to the wrath of God because of sin. The cup that Jesus was referring to was the cup of trembling (judgment). For there to be salvation, sin had to be judged. Jesus, as the Lamb of God, was about to take upon Himself the judgment of God for the sins of all mankind—the punishment of God's wrath appointed to sinners. Isaiah 51:22 says, *"Thus saith thy Lord the LORD, and thy God that pleadeth the cause of his people, Behold, I have taken out of thine hand the cup of trembling, even the dregs of the cup of my fury; thou shalt no more drink it again."* Psalm 75:8 says, *"For in the hand of the LORD there is a cup, and the wine is red; it is full of mixture; and he poureth out of the same: but the dregs thereof, all the wicked of the earth shall wring them out, and drink them."* Psalm 116:13 says, *"I will take the cup of salvation, and call upon the name of the LORD."*

As Jesus prayed, the intensity of His burden grew into travail. Why? Could it be because He could hear the cries of countless lost souls pleading for the cup of judgment to pass from them? Could He have seen a vision of all the spirits in *hades* waiting for the promise of redemption?

Travail in and of itself is a birthing process. His burden for Jew and Gentile alike caused Him to travail until the church was birthed into the kingdom of God. Isaiah 53:11-12 confirms the purpose of His agonizing, travailing prayer in the garden: *"He shall see of the travail of his soul, and*

*shall be satisfied: by his knowledge shall my righteous servant justify
many; for he shall bear their iniquities. Therefore will I divide him a
portion with the great, and he shall divide the spoil with the strong;
because he hath poured out his soul unto death: and he was numbered
with the transgressors; and he bare the sin of many, and made intercession for the transgressors."*

Jesus submitted to the burden of the Spirit in the
Garden of Gethsemane. We are the present-day fruit of His
travail. Today, we are living in the divine overflow of His
intercession made in the garden.

We are quickly approaching midnight. The powers of
darkness are advancing faster than ever before. Every sign
in heaven and earth is pointing to the eastern sky and the
soon return of our Lord. We must watch and pray and not
sleep. We must awaken to realize the urgency of the hour.
Jesus could have slept with His disciples, but the burden
wouldn't let Him rest. He wrestled in prayer until He
prayed through the burden of the Spirit. We, too, must
wrestle in prayer for all the souls that are dying and going
to hell. Time is short and the only earthly treasure that has
any eternal value is a soul.

Over and over again, we see the importance of a burden realized in the Word of God. Abraham had a burden
for Sodom and Gomorrah. He prayed and Lot was saved.
Jacob wrestled all night with the angel of the Lord, and
his name was changed from Jacob (supplanter) to Israel
(prince with God). Moses cried out to God, *"if thou wilt
forgive their sin——; and if not, blot me, I pray thee, out of thy book*

which thou hast written" (Exodus 32:32). King David had a burden for his enemies. Psalms 35:13-14 reads, "But as for me, when they were sick my clothing became sackcloth: I humbled my soul with fasting; and my prayer returned into mine bosom. I behaved myself as though he had been my friend or brother: I bowed down heavily, as one that mourneth for his mother." Nehemiah received a burden after hearing about the desolation of Jerusalem. He fasted and prayed certain days, repenting and making supplication for the whole nation. This resulted in God using him to rebuild the city.

What is a Burden?

Webster's Dictionary defines a burden as "that which is borne with labor or difficulty; that which is grievous, wearisome, or oppressive. The bearing of loads; a birth, also a child in the womb."

When we agree to yoke ourselves with the burden of the Lord's heart, we are taking up our cross and following Him. Our job is to pray the burden of the heart of God. We do this until it lifts from us.

God does everything through the spoken word. When God has a burden, He looks for a person to speak it and to birth it into existence. God then manifests His creative response to the burden openly.

Reverend Teklemariam Gezahagne said, "Fasting is not only pleading, but it is a bleeding of the heart; this produces brokenhearted saints. Out of all giving, fasting and prayer are the most important! We need to pray and draw nigh the mercy of God into the nations that are dying. God will not ignore a broken heart."

Hosea 6:6 says, *"For I desired mercy, and not sacrifice; and the knowledge of God more than burnt offerings."*

> *If I have not a burden for lost souls*
> *then I am not a Christian.*
> TEKLEMARIAM GEZAHAGNE

In Isaiah 59, we see the state of a nation that failed to recognize the importance of a burden. They were so busy in their daily affairs that God could not find anyone who would carry the burden of His heart so that justice and judgment could be restored to the city.

Even today, truth is falling in our streets, and judgment is turned back. Truth and justice no longer rule the hearts and minds of people. *"None calleth for justice, nor any pleadeth for truth: they trust in vanity, and speak lies; they conceive mischief, and bring forth iniquity"* (Isaiah 59:4). The burden of God was to restore and to save, but no one would take heed to His heartbeat.

Let us stoop down and yoke ourselves with the heart-beat of Jesus. In light of eternity we will never know how often our stooping has pulled souls out of a devil's hell.

Jesus is the great intercessor, Whose eyes scan all the earth seeking someone who will pray—someone through whom He can show himself strong. Jesus is going to use someone to fast and pray His burden; it may as well be you, and it may as well be me.

Chapter Six

GOALS AND HINDRANCES

Goals During a Fast

As previously mentioned, you must have a burden and purpose when you fast. If you are not clear why you are fasting, pray and ask God to impress your heart with a purpose. After establishing a purpose, you can set a goal for your fast. Make sure your purpose and goal are scripturally sound. Isaiah 58 is a good guideline for checking your motives and establishing your purpose.

Although your purpose will change for each fast, brokenness of heart, repentance, and the salvation of souls are God's first priorities.

Put aside time to maintain prayer and Bible reading when you fast. Prayer and the Word will strengthen and sustain you throughout your fast. Because fasting is a time of abstinence unto the Lord, when possible, spend extra time praying and meditating on the Word. It is beneficial to search the Scriptures before you fast and to choose passages you can pray and meditate on while you are fasting. It is a good idea to set aside normal mealtimes for communion with Jesus while fasting.

The Word is sustenance (food) for our spiritual man. Eating a balanced diet from the Word of God and drinking from the living waters of the Spirit (prayer) will help you develop a strong walk with God. Daniel said, *"The people that do know their God shall be strong, and do exploits"* (Daniel 11:32).

Hindrances to Fasting

If you have headaches while fasting, decrease your intake of caffeine and eat foods with fewer additives (monosodium glutamate has been known to cause headaches). You can help reduce diarrhea and stomach problems by eating carefully before and after a fast. To avoid constipation and difficulty urinating during the fast do not drink apple, grape, or orange juice from concentrate, or soy milk.

Oftentimes, your prayer life may seem hindered while fasting. This is because you are releasing toxins and bringing your flesh under subjection to the Spirit. You are also fighting unseen powers that are trying to hinder the results of your fast. Therefore, the most important thing to do is *"press on!"* Do not be discouraged if you do not see results during your fast. Most of the time, the results will come after you have completed the fast.

Weakness and hunger are a part of fasting. The Word of God says, *"If we suffer, we shall also reign with him"* (II Timothy 2:12). The Word also says, *"He that hath suffered in the flesh hath ceased from sin"* (I Peter 4:1). It is important to understand that although it appears you're dying in the natural, you are actually coming to life in the spiritual. You may also feel the need to rest at unusual times throughout the day. Take the time and do so if you can. You may find your energy is needed for prayer or meditation at times throughout the night.

Chapter Seven

TYPES OF FASTS

There are several different ways you can fast. The list below has been taken from Joy Haney's book *When Ye Fast.* I highly recommend this book to anyone who wants to develop a lifestyle of fasting in their walk with God.

- No food or water
  (One to three days, but never more than three days.)
- Water only
- Water, honey, and lemon
  (Honey and lemon are natural cleansers for your body. The honey will also give you strength. This is a good three-day cleansing fast.)
- Juice
  (No food, only juice. Fruit juices should not be mixed with vegetable juices. Fruit juices should not be made with sugar.)

- Combination
  (Take juices with an addition of hot herbal tea with honey.)
- Daniel's ten-day fast
  (Eat pulse [grains, lentils, and vegetables] and water only.)
- Daniel's twenty-one-day fast
  (Do not eat bread, desserts, juices, or meat.)
- Drink water for three days then have broth for strength on day 4
  (Repeat this sequence until the fast is complete.)

Here are two recipes for broth used during longer fasts:

(1) Gently boil carrots, onions, parsley, and spinach (only until softened but still dark green). Put all in blender and blend into a broth to drink.

(2) Do the same as above, but instead use tomatoes, carrots, sautéed garlic, and onion.

It is good to end a fast with grape juice. *Slowly* start back into eating with fruits, cooked vegetables, and toast.

TIPS

All of the fasts listed here are biblical. Determine the type of fast you want to undertake—and then do it! You may want to do a combination fast, starting with water and ending with vegetables. Go for it! *The most important thing to do is start.* Do not be afraid. The Lord will help you learn as you fast! If you have a job that requires heavy physical labor, you will find that the vegetable broths help increase your strength. If you feel faint, rest and drink some fresh juice or honey-lemon water. Vegetable juice broth is best if you are sensitive to sugar. Avoid excessive amounts of any type of liquid except water. *Drink a lot of water!*

Chapter Eight

FASTING AND YOUR HEALTH

Nutrition

Good nutrition is not a twenty-first-century revelation that is sweeping America. This revelation existed in the Garden of Eden. God Himself looked at all the trees He had created for food and saw that they were good! God created all the foods necessary to produce a nutritionally balanced diet. He then reemphasized nutrition through dietary laws written for the Jewish people under the law. Although the Lord used the dietary laws to differentiate between clean and unclean, scientific studies have proven that there are parasites within unclean animals that can be harmful to the human body.

To prove how important the proper diet is to a believer, let us take a look at the life of Daniel. In Daniel 1, the first step the king took to assimilate the Hebrew children into the Babylonian culture was to change their diet. *"And the king appointed them a daily provision of the king's meat, and of the wine which he drank: so nourishing them three years, that at the end thereof they might stand before the king"* (Daniel 1:5). In virtually every culture, food is used as a means of assimilation into that culture.

Now, Daniel and the three Hebrew young men were the only four mentioned, out of all the young men brought into the king's palace, who purposed in their hearts not to compromise the laws of God for the favor of man. Because of this, God gave Daniel favor with the prince of the eunuchs. This resulted in his granting Daniel's request to eat "pulse" (vegetables) and to drink water for ten days. The results were glorious. Daniel 1:15 reads, *"And at the end of ten days their countenances appeared fairer and fatter in flesh than all the children which did eat the portion of the king's meat."* The Word goes on to say that *"as for these four children, God gave them knowledge and skill in all learning and wisdom: and Daniel had understanding in all visions and dreams."*

The young men who compromised their convictions are never mentioned in the Bible. They ended up assimilating into the Babylonian culture and forsaking the commandments of God.

Nutrition plays a very active role in keeping our temples consecrated to the Lord. Much of what we call food is in reality fat, sugar, and chemicals that are producing dangerous chemical and psychological imbalances within our bodies. These imbalances affect not only our physical endurance and productivity but also our mental abilities to process information, concentrate, and make decisions. All of these are necessary for producing God's blessings in our lives and for helping us to be the best we can be for God.

Many of our physical illnesses can be completely cured by proper nutrition and fasting. Isaiah 58:8 teaches us that fasting brings forth healing speedily.

What is the King's Meat Today?

Fast Foods

There does not need to be a lot of explanation about what fast foods are. The Word teaches us that anything done in haste comes to nothing. This is true with our eating habits also. Fast foods provide little nutritional value for our body. The only real benefit is that they satisfy hunger pangs temporarily. Have you ever noticed that the more junk food you eat, the more you want to eat? This is because your body is being stimulated by the fats and additives in fast foods. Therefore, it is not receiving the important nutrients it needs to be satisfied. In addition, eating fast foods builds up toxins (poisons) in your body. This makes fasting more difficult because of the physical hardship experienced while the body is cleansing itself of these poisons.

Fasting alters the way you think about food. After cleansing your body on a fast, you are less likely to want to refill it with junk. You always can return to old habits, but it's better to start new ones. If you are going to eat out, either choose healthier fast foods, or invest in a balanced meal at a more formal restaurant. At all other times, prepare nutritious meals at home and eat what is prepared. This will save a significant amount of money and headaches (unnecessary suffering)!

Processed and Fat-Free Foods

Processed foods are foods that have been altered in some way from their original state. These alterations improve the shelf life of food, but they often destroy the nutritional value of that food. Many of the chemicals found in processed foods have been found to be cancer-causing and addictive. In addition, many processed foods contain high quantities of sugars that have numerous, unhealthy side effects.

It is wiser to invest in fresh ingredients, fresh food, and the extra time needed to prepare meals in larger quantities. Leftovers can be easily frozen in individual meal sizes. This is not only cost-effective, but it's much more nutritious and satisfying.

Fat-free foods do not alter a person's eating habits. Rarely do people who eat fat-free foods lose the weight desired, and what they sacrifice in calories, they gain in chemicals. It is wiser to eat purer food products and simply cut back on how much is eaten.

Soda

I remember a time, many years ago, when my car died in the parking lot of my workplace. Upon examination, I found that the battery cables were corroded. Therefore, I took baking soda and a toothbrush and proceeded to clean the cables. While I was cleaning them, a girlfriend suggested using Coke. So I tried it. To my amazement the Coke dissolved the corrosion immediately, the car started, and off I went! Can you imagine what soda can do to a stomach? The ingredients of soda are water, artificial colorings and flavorings, and sugar. The diet brands contain cancer-causing agents such as saccharin or NutraSweet. For a soda alternative, try combining fruit juice with soda water (carbonated water). It is refreshing, tastes great, and is nutritious. (Note: The above does not pertain to the necessary sugar restrictions of diabetics.)

Caffeine

There are some benefits to caffeine. It produces increased mental alertness. It stimulates the burning of extra calories. For those with breathing problems, it serves as a respiratory relaxer, and it can increase blood flow. However, there are also other important facts to consider when consuming caffeine.

First, caffeine is a drug, and it is addictive. It also has been associated with heart disease, birth defects, digestive disorders, breast cancer, fever, headaches, and anxiety. In addition, it has been associated with depression. Caffeine also releases insulin. Insulin causes blood sugar to drop which in turn creates hunger pangs.

You need to get control over anything that is currently controlling you. Those who consume large quantities of caffeine often find it more difficult to fast. Fasting is a cleansing process—physically and spiritually. Therefore, as toxins are being eliminated from your body, there can be side effects such as headaches, nausea, shakes, anxiety, etc. These side effects have discouraged some from fasting. The withdrawal from caffeine can cause numerous side effects, but those who have kicked the caffeine habit feel better physically and emotionally.

There are ways to break the caffeine habit. When you want a quick pick-me-up, try hot water with lemon and honey. There are also grain-based products such as Postum and Pero that taste similar to coffee. They are low in calories and are made from bran, wheat, and molasses. Cafix is another grain-based drink that can be purchased either in a supermarket or health-food store. Caffeine-free coffee and herbal tea are good alternatives, although it has been documented that herbal teas can be a more serious health hazard than coffee. Fruit and vegetable juices are also good alternatives to caffeinated drinks.

Note: moderation and good eating habits are the keys to enjoying a lifestyle of fasting and good health. For those who enjoy drinking caffeinated products, such as coffee, let moderation be your guide. The more you minimize your intake, the better you will feel overall.

"Can you fast by drinking coffee, soda, etc., and if so, does God consider it a valid fast?" The answer is *yes* to both questions, unless God has dealt with you otherwise. However, I do not recommend fasting this way. Fasting is a time of purification; water and juices are best suited for fasting. Putting nutritionally poor substances into your body could result in symptoms of diabetes, hypoglycemia, and other chemical imbalances. It is best to train yourself to fast with water and/or fresh juices.

Refined Flours

Refined flours lack approximately 80 percent of essential nutrients found in whole-grain flours. Whole-grain flours contain many B vitamins that aid in the absorption and metabolism of proteins; they also help the body use fats and assist in the formation of red blood cells. Whole-grain flours also contain vegetable oil and vitamin E, as well as protein.

Many people buy breads made with refined flours because they cost less, and the "kids" like them better. Although this may be partially true, you can usually find good whole-grain bread at reduced prices in your local store. You may even want to consider making your own bread. It does take extra time, but it can be cost-effective, and your family will love it.

Buying nutritionally deficient foods to save money is a myth because these types of foods do not satisfy the body's nutritional needs, and therefore the body requires and craves more food. Consequently, you will spend more money on food because of increased food consumption.

Sugar

Sugar is this nation's most popular food additive. We

consume ten times more sugar than all the other 2,600 or so food additives combined, except salt (a distant second). Next time you go shopping, check the ingredient lists on the processed foods you buy and count how many of them contain sugar.

The only benefit of sugar is the calories: only four per gram. There is not enough time to describe the ill effects of sugar. Let it suffice to say that excessive sugar intake can affect you physically, socially, and mentally. Many of the disturbing emotional problems today's children suffer from could be corrected by reducing the amount of sugar in their diets. The severe concentration problems among Americans today could most assuredly be reversed by diet. The saddest thing that sugar does to your body is that it destroys many of the important nutrients your body processes after eating. This results in a weakened immune system, among other things.

To Cut Down on Sugar:

1. Cut back on stocking sweets and candy at home. Instead, provide fresh fruits and vegetables. Popcorn is also a healthy snack.

2. Get in the habit of serving fruit. Fresh fruit can quench the most ferocious sweet attack if you will reach for it instead of a sweet. You can also cook fruit to make it sweeter tasting; add honey and you have a dessert.

3. Bake your own cakes and sweets at home. Cut the sugar called for by one-third to one-half. You will find your

baking more satisfying and healthier.

Where Do You Begin?

Moderation Is the Key

Begin by praying and asking God to direct you into a lifestyle of eating that pleases Him. Start fasting one to three days a week to rid your body of toxins that have accumulated over time and that are poisoning your body.

Start planning meals, including desserts. Purchase only the necessary ingredients to make these meals. Buy more fresh vegetables and fruits. Replace excessive use of red meat with moderate portions of chicken or fish. Buy whole-grain breads. Stock up on staple foods such as grains, spices, potatoes (a great nutritional investment), rice, onions, garlic, oil, etc.

Read up on nutrition. There is a great deal of information available to the public on nutrition. I was asked to include a section on nutrition in this book. I have only touched on the basics and, therefore, recommend that you look into other resources. Joy Haney has written a book entitled *Radiant Health*. Nona Freeman has also written a book entitled *Keeper of the House*. Both of these books are highly recommended and contain valuable information that will bless you for years to come.

Jane Brody's *Good Food Book* and *Nutrition Book* are two outstanding resources for nutritional information and meal planning. Her books contain excellent low-fat recipes and cooking tips that will enhance any kitchen. Many of the facts presented in this nutrition section have been gleaned from Jane Brody's *Nutrition Book*.

Another highly recommended book is *Eat Right for Your Type*, written by Dr. Peter J. D'Adamo. This book enlightens you on foods and dietary guidelines that are compatible with your blood type. Although eating a healthful way has its nutritional benefits, not everyone can eat the same foods and maintain their weight and energy level. For example, a person with type-O blood is benefited by a high-protein, low-carbohydrate diet, while a person with type-A blood is benefited by a vegetarian diet, or high-carbohydrate and low-protein diet. You will find this book to be genuinely refreshing and helpful in establishing better eating habits.

Finally, make nutrition a family affair. Get everyone involved in the planning, cooking, and serving of meals. Try new and different recipes. Study Scriptures pertaining to food and dietary customs in the Bible. Once you and your family get a taste of the real thing, you will find yourselves eating better, feeling better, and fasting better!

Exercise, in its Place

Exercise aids in the cleansing process a body goes through while on a fast. Besides being a present-day craze in our society, exercise is necessary because of our sedentary lifestyles. As Christians, we must keep exercise in its proper perspective. One rule of thumb I endeavor to live by is, *"Do not do for your body what you will not do for God."* Many of us will spend precious time, resources, and strength to be physically fit, and yet our spiritual man is frail, flabby, weak, and starving from malnutrition. The benefits of spending time with Jesus far exceed any earthly or fleshly gain!

Prior to being born again, I was a certified health and fitness consultant. When I came to the Lord, I was in training for a triathlon. This endeavor required working out at home or in a health club a minimum of two to four hours a day, five to six days per week. After coming to the Lord, I purposed in my heart to invest the same amount of time in prayer. I found that prayer within itself was (and still is) good exercise for the body. *Many* (not all) saints would not have excessive weight problems if they gave themselves to the basics of the kingdom: prayer, fasting, and the study of God's Word.

Exercise does have its benefits and should become a part of your daily life to some extent, but it should never exceed the time and energy given to your personal relationship with Jesus. Proverbs 31:30 sums up all that can be said regarding any issue of personal vanity: *"Favour is deceitful, and beauty is vain: but a woman [or man] that feareth the LORD, she [he] shall be praised."*

There are those who struggle in the area of weight control, as well as fasting and prayer. It is important to understand that there are weaknesses in all of our lives. A weakness can only become a strength and a victory report through God's unfailing mercy and His unlimited grace (divine assistance). When we learn how to yield to God in the face of weakness, then we are on the road to overcoming all things. Fasting can be compared to a bulldozer removing everything in its path so the road can be built. Fasting is a very helpful tool in overcoming any yoke of bondage. At one time, I struggled with gaining weight, and I was in bondage to sweets (in particular chocolate). This resulted in slothfulness, mental dullness, and uncontrolled eating habits. Through fasting, much prayer, and praying for others with the same problem, deliverance came. The Lord lifted my addiction to chocolate, and I have not had a piece of chocolate for more than eight years! To God be the glory! *The Lord is no respecter of persons . . . He will set you free, too!*

Weight control and exercise are only important in relationship to your physical well-being and life span here on earth. As a member of the kingdom of God, you are not judged according to your physical appearance (this is how the world judges you), but you are judged according to your spiritual appearance. Are you adorned in holiness and clothed in meekness? Are the wisdom and power of Jesus demonstrated in your life? Do you have an excellent spirit like Joseph or Daniel? Is your outward appearance modest? Do people see and hear Jesus when they meet you?

The words penned in Romans 14:3 and 13 clearly reveal God's perspective on the whole matter of eating, exercising, etc. Understanding and acting on these inspired words will cause us to enter into the seventh dimension of God's kingdom: Love.

> *Let not him that eateth despise him that eateth not;*
> *and let not him which eateth not judge him that eateth:*
> *for God hath received him. . . . So then every one of us*
> *shall give account of himself to God. Let us not therefore*
> *judge one another any more: but judge this rather,*
> *that no man put a stumbling block or an occasion*
> *to fall in his brother's way.*
> ROMANS 14:3, 12-13

Beneficial Exercises

Walking is one of the best exercises. If you choose to walk, walk at least twenty minutes at a time. (It takes twenty minutes of continuous aerobic exercise to increase your metabolic rate.) This will help your metabolism and blood circulation as well as strengthen your cardiovascular system and your muscles. You can also combine your prayer time with walking. Go on a prayer walk. Find a quiet area and just talk to Jesus while you are walking. Before you know it, you will have prayed an hour and exercised, too!

If you enjoy aerobics and/or body building, there are Christian exercise tapes available that enable you to exercise in the privacy of your own home. If you choose to work out at a health club, choose the club carefully. I do not advise memberships to coed health clubs. The primary reason is

that the level of immodesty and sensual influence contra-
dicts biblical modesty, as well as the scriptural admonition
to abstain from all fleshly lusts that war against the soul. In
addition, oftentimes the spiritual environment of certain
health clubs is not conducive to the spiritual growth of a
Christian. There are health clubs that cater only to women
or only to men. You may want to consider these types of
facilities when choosing a health club.

Chapter Nine

SCRIPTURES FOR MEDITATION

The following scriptures have been compiled to help you stay focused while fasting. Take time to read them and meditate on them before and during a fast. You will find strength in the Word.

But put ye on the Lord Jesus Christ, and make not provision
for the flesh, to fulfil the lusts thereof.
ROMANS 13:14

Draw nigh to God, and he will draw nigh to you. Cleanse your
hands, ye sinners; and purify your hearts, ye double minded.
Be afflicted, and mourn, and weep: let your laughter be turned
to mourning, and your joy to heaviness. Humble yourselves
in the sight of the Lord, and he shall lift you up.
JAMES 4:8-10

I am crucified with Christ: nevertheless I live; yet not I,
but Christ liveth in me: and the life which I now live in the flesh

I live by the faith of the Son of God, who loved me,
and gave himself for me.

GALATIANS 2:20

I beseech you therefore, brethren, by the mercies of God,
that ye present your bodies a living sacrifice, holy, acceptable
unto God, which is your reasonable service. And be not conformed
to this world: but be ye transformed by the renewing of your mind,
that ye may prove what is that good, and acceptable,
and perfect, will of God.

ROMANS 12:1-2

Let not sin therefore reign in your mortal body,
that ye should obey it in the lusts thereof.

ROMANS 6:12

Moreover when ye fast, be not, as the hypocrites,
of a sad countenance: for they disfigure their faces,
that they may appear unto men to fast. Verily I say unto you,
They have their reward. But thou, when thou fastest,
anoint thine head, and wash thy face;
that thou appear not unto men to fast,
but unto thy Father which is in secret:
and thy Father, which seeth in secret,
shall reward thee openly.

MATTHEW 6:16-18

Then came the disciples to Jesus apart, and said,
Why could not we cast him out? And Jesus said unto them,
Because of your unbelief: for verily I say unto you,
If ye have faith as a grain of mustard seed,
ye shall say unto this mountain, Remove hence to yonder place;
and it shall remove; and nothing shall be impossible unto you.
Howbeit this kind goeth not out but by prayer and fasting.
(Prayer and fasting purges unbelief and releases faith
that moves mountains!)
MATTHEW 17:19-21

Let nothing be done through strife or vainglory; but in lowliness
of mind let each esteem other better than themselves.
(Fasting should humble your soul.
This Scripture can be used in conjunction with Isaiah 58:9.)
PHILIPPIANS 2:3

Forasmuch then as Christ hath suffered for us in the flesh,
arm yourselves likewise with the same mind:
for he that hath suffered in the flesh hath ceased from sin;
that he no longer should live the rest of his time in the flesh
to the lusts of men, but to the will of God.
I PETER 4:1-2

Part Two

PRAYER

AUTHOR'S NOTE

There are many people today who spend countless hours "surfing the 'Net" to gain knowledge in any and every conceivable area of life. The knowledge that is accessed through the Internet is seemingly inexhaustible— but it's only temporal.

Yet, there is another Internet that few people ever surf. It is the Internet of the Spirit: the knowledge of Jesus Christ and His kingdom. It is divine, inexhaustible—and eternal. When one learns to "surf God's 'Net," he or she becomes God-conscious and obtains knowledge that can be used to lift a fallen world, not destroy it.

May your prayer life be stirred and enriched as you read the second part of this book. May the Lord shine His countenance on you and cause you to reach new heights in your relationship with Him.

Chapter One

THE DIVINE
FIRST OF ALL

*I exhort therefore, that, first of all, supplications, prayers,
intercessions, and giving of thanks, be made for all men.*
I TIMOTHY 2:1

Prayer was the catalyst that birthed the early apostolic church. It was a critical part of the apostolic lifestyle. There would not be an apostolic church if there had not been a Pentecost, and there would not have been a Pentecost without prayer! Acts 1:14 says, *"These all continued with one accord in prayer and supplication."*

Prayer brought forth the fulfillment of the promise (John 14:26; Acts 2:38-39), and the promise empowered the disciples, who *"continued stedfastly in the apostles' doctrine and fellowship, and in breaking of bread, and in **prayers.**"*

The early church was known for its fervency in prayer. The church prayed without ceasing, and as a result, all of Jerusalem was filled with apostolic doctrine. They ceased not to teach and preach Jesus Christ in every home. The

85

power, the glory, and the fear of God filled the lifestyle of every saint.

Today, prayer is still the catalyst that brings true revival to any church, city, or nation. We can look back to Azusa Street and find prayer birthing the twentieth-century outpouring of the Holy Ghost. It was the fervent prayer of a young man, Evan Roberts, which was the catalyst for the great Welsh revival. This revival spread throughout South Wales and as far as New Zealand. Noon-hour prayer meetings changed the course of sinful cities in America and Ireland during the mid-1800s.

It was fervent, united prayer during Finney's revivals that ushered in such conviction of sin that entire factories were shut down to give employees time to repent and be converted. Yes, we can read about men such as these who changed nations through prayer, but we need to experience it for ourselves!

Today there are those among us who are changing the course of lives in churches, cities, and nations through prayer. I can still hear Erkenesh Gezahagne saying, "One hour of prayer will only keep you from temptation, two hours of prayer will give you power with God." The result of her intercession is a church in Ethiopia with more than one million members today. Shirley Cole has given her life to intercession, and the result has been hundreds of thousands of souls filled with the Holy Ghost through her husband's ministry, throughout the world.

Reverend Andrew Bar David Urshan said, "Give me an

assembly of saints who pray more than they dance and sing; who pray more than visiting; who pray more than talking about each other, and who pray with a holy life behind their prayers, and I will show you in truth an assembly of God where He actually talks and works miracles. So the secret of working miracles that Jesus and His apostles wrought is a cleansed life first; a cleansed temple second; then praying, praying, praying, because, *'It is written, My house shall be called the house of prayer'"* (Matthew 21:13).

Prayer is an art. It is one of the five senses of God's Spirit—Faith, Hope, Reverence, Worship, Prayer—and like any one of the five senses it has to be developed by use. Prayer is directly connected to your reasoning and logic. The more you pray, the more you will cast off the logic of this world and put on the mind of Christ. You will leave the world of self-consciousness and enter into the world of God-consciousness. It is in this state of being that you will truly walk in the spirit with God.

Chapter Two

WHAT IS PRAYER?

*Be careful for nothing; but in every thing by prayer and supplication
with thanksgiving let your requests be made known unto God.*
PHILIPPIANS 4:6

Conversation

Prayer is having a conversation with God. It is the means by which you "seek after God" and develop a relationship with Him. As you know, a conversation can take many different directions. There are short conversations and long conversations; intellectual conversations and brainless conversations; deep, intimate, conversations or lighthearted conversations. There are spiritual conversations and not-so-spiritual conversations. No matter what type of conversation it is, to really get to know a person you have to spend time communicating with that person. Have you ever called a friend and patiently endured several interruptions before you were able to finish your conversation? How much more fruitful would that conversation have

been if it had been focused and not interrupted! You may
have discovered that the more time you spend with someone the easier it is to communicate with that person. Once
honest, heart-to-heart communication begins between two
people it can manifest different depths throughout the
conversation. For example, in one conversation you can
laugh together, cry together, be serious together, dream
together, agree and disagree together, and when the conversation is through, you feel that you've accomplished something together.

Prayer is the contact point of conversation between us
and God. It can take several different directions such as
thanksgiving, worship, supplication (humble petition), and
intercession. It enables you to get to know each other.
I Corinthians 13:12 says, *"But then shall I know even as also I
am known."* Could it be that the more you let God into your
life and express your heart to Him through prayer, the more
God will let you into His life and express His heart to you
in prayer?

What Will Prayer Do for You?

It will:
- Develop your relationship with God (Job 23:3-5)
- Build your faith (Jude 20)
- Bring direction (Proverbs 3:5-6)
- Give you favor (Luke 2:52; Acts 7:10)
- Convict you of sin (Job 13:23; Psalm 139:23-24)
- Renew your spirit (Psalm 51)

- Save your soul (Luke 21:36)
- Increase your obedience (Psalm 119; Matthew 7:21)
- Sanctify (purify) your soul (Psalm 17:5; 19:12)
- Sanctify your food and water (I Timothy 4:4-5)
- Make provision for your needs (Matthew 6:33-34)
- Help in the time of trouble (Psalm 34:4-6; Acts 12:5)
- Deliver you from fears (Psalm 34:4)
- Deliver you from your enemies (Psalm 64)
- Help you overcome temptation (Hebrews 4:15-16)
- Bring peace (Philippians 4:6-7)
- Bring success in business (I Chronicles 4:10)
- Bring healing (Psalm 6:2-9; 103:2-3)
- Make you a soulwinner (Psalm 2:8)
- Enable you to do exploits (Daniel 11:32)
- Give you favor in old age (Psalm 71:9)
- Usher in the kingdom of God (Righteousness, Joy, and Peace) (Matthew 6:10)
- Change the course of nations (Daniel 6:11-26)
- Change the course of eternity (Matthew 26:46)

The Key Ingredient

Whether you're developing a relationship, preparing a meal, baking a cake, fixing a car, running an errand, or writing an essay, there is one key ingredient needed: time! Getting to know Jesus requires spending time with Him. Spending time with Him develops your ability to communicate with Him. Effective communication requires not only talking but also listening. This ability is acquired by learning how to flow in and with the Spirit of God. Acts 17:28 states, *"For in him we live, and move, and have our being."* John 15:7 says, *"If you abide in me, and my words abide in you, ye shall ask what ye will, and it shall be done unto you."* *Webster's Dictionary* defines *abide* as "a state of waiting patiently, enduring without yielding, to accept without objection, or to continue in a place." You can learn to abide in and communicate with Jesus; it just takes time!

It is important to establish a time and place of prayer. Jesus rose up early every morning to pray. Morning is a good time to commune with the Lord. The early morning hours are generally calm and peaceful, enabling you to pray with minimal distraction. Psalm 5:3 says, *"My voice shalt thou hear in the morning, O LORD; in the morning will I direct my prayer unto thee, and will look up."* And Psalm 55:17 says, *"Evening, and morning, and at noon, will I pray, and cry aloud: and he shall hear my voice."* If you are unable to pray in the mornings, work out an uninterrupted time and place of prayer some other time during the day.

Chapter Three

THE RIVER PRINCIPLE

And he shewed me a pure river of water of life, clear as crystal, proceeding out of the throne of God and of the Lamb.

REVELATION 22:1

The Principle

Reverend Nathaniel Haney describes prayer as being much like the flow of a river. All rivers have a starting point and usually end up flowing into a larger body of water. As you follow a river's edge you will observe that the river curves, taking on different depths and widths. You may have noticed that where a river is wide and deep the water does not appear to be moving. Yet, as the river bed becomes narrower and shallower, you will see the current with the same amount of water begin to churn. As it churns, it turns into what is called "white water" or rapids. White water moves with great force and swiftness. As you near the end of the white water, the flow of the river appears to slow as the river begins to deepen, producing a refreshing quietness and stillness.

The quality of time you spend in prayer can be dra-matically increased by learning how to flow in the river of God's Spirit. At times in prayer, it will seem as if you are not moving at all, and yet at other times, it's as if you are rafting through white water. It is in these contrasting times of quietness and exhilaration that you learn how to flow with the Spirit of God.

Often, after an exhilarating move of the Spirit, you will find yourself winding down into a time of quietness and calmness in the Holy Ghost. At this point you may mis-takenly think that you are through praying—you're not, hold on! Though it may appear to be a stopping point, this is often the time that God desires to speak to you. You have entered into a place in the Spirit that even though the waters are still, the river is still moving, and the waters are deep.

In this deep, still place God speaks to your heart. As you wait, He may impress a thought or a Scripture on your heart for you to meditate on. You will also experience a renewal of your strength, for it is written, *"But they that wait upon the LORD shall renew their strength; they shall mount up with wings as eagles; they shall run, and not be weary; and they shall walk, and not faint"* (Isaiah 40:31). Your mind will be renewed, and you will take hold of God's promises as you gently float in the river of God's Spirit. If you stay there long enough, the river's intensity will escalate again and push you on through more white water of the Spirit until you find your-

self in another quiet cove of glory, nestled in the heart of
God.

> *If you can learn this principle of prayer,*
> *you can spend all day in prayer.*

How to Get into the River

There are two ways to get into a river. You can either
wade in slowly or jump right in. It is the same when you
are entering into the river of the Spirit. There will be times
when you enter slowly through praise and worship, and
then there will be times when you jump right in with intercession. In either case, you always enter into the river with
an attitude of humility and holy reverence. When you
humble yourself in His presence, He will lift you into His
glory.

As your spirit unites with His, be sensitive to the
impressions placed upon your spirit. Worship may lead you
into a season of repentance, which may lead you into a time
of weeping and supplication (humble petition) for your
needs and the needs of others. Then a shift in the Spirit
may come, and you may begin to intercede for your city or
nation. Your intercession may be followed with a calm and
quiet time. During this time, the Lord desires to talk with
you. He may impress a song or Scripture upon your heart.
He may give you a promise or revelation as you wait upon
him. After a time of quietness, you may feel the Spirit
beginning to stir you again. Jesus may drop a need into

your heart and suddenly you're again riding the white water of intercession. The moanings and groanings of travail may overtake your heart until you feel a release. After a breakthrough, you will find yourself, once again, nestled in a quiet place with God, receiving strength to move ahead.

When you learn to flow in the river of God's Spirit, you will find there is a place in the Spirit where you can minister to the Lord. The Bible is full of examples of those who ministered to the Lord. Acts 13:2 mentions, *"As they ministered to the Lord . . ."* Deuteronomy 10:8 states, *"At that time the LORD separated the tribe of Levi, to bear the ark of the covenant of the LORD, to stand before the LORD to minister unto him, and to bless in his name, unto this day."* I Samuel 3:1 says, *"And the child Samuel ministered unto the LORD before Eli."*

In what ways can you minister to the Lord?
- Whatever the present need of the Lord is, you can help carry that burden in prayer.
- Talk to Him not only about His mighty acts, but also about His commandments and His ways.
- Meditate in His Word day and night. *Meditate* means "to speak to oneself repetitively."
- You fulfill the highest purpose of your creation when you love Him and worship Him.

To reiterate, prayer is a conversation with God. Sometimes it's quiet and still, and at other times it's so exhilarating you can hardly contain yourself. Sometimes you are ministering to the Lord, and sometimes the Lord is ministering to you! When you are involved in prayer, you are involved in a real relationship with a real God Who can hear you, see you, talk with you, and touch you with His divine presence!

John 7:37-39 says, "*In the last day, that great day of the feast, Jesus stood and cried, saying, If any man thirst, let him come unto me, and drink. He that believeth on me, as the scripture hath said, out of his belly shall flow rivers of living water. (But this spake he of the Spirit, which they that believe on him should receive: for the Holy Ghost was not yet given; because that Jesus was not yet glorified.)*"

Chapter Four

DISCIPLINE

And the man Jeroboam was a mighty man of valour:
and Solomon seeing the young man that he was industrious,
he made him ruler over all the charge of the house of Joseph.

I KINGS 11:28

Self-Discipline

In today's society, self-discipline may be one of the most misunderstood and often scoffed at principles of life. Yet, the more you are self-disciplined, the more you will realize your dreams and accomplish your goals. Self-discipline develops confidence, efficiency, and order within your lifestyle. It also creates a much healthier outlook on life. It's time to take the word *self-discipline* off the list of the ten most unwanted traits in your life and place it on the top of the list of the ten most desired attributes in your life.

Do you want to be Spirit-led? The more disciplined you are in the ways of God, the more Spirit-led you will be. A Spirit-led life is a life yielded to the leading and voice of

God's Spirit. If you struggle with obedience to God's Word in your life, it is because you are warring between your flesh and your mind. It's time to discipline yourself to the Word and Spirit of God. The Word of God is the map that tells you how to get from point A to point B. The more you study the map, the easier it will be for you to know how to get where you want to go. A great way to start is by meditating on and memorizing passages in Romans 6, 7, and 8.

Self-discipline has the potential to cause you to pray, fast, read the Word, witness, keep a clean and orderly house, set goals and reach them, eat well, think clearly, think quickly, control your emotions, and have more energy— consistently.

Webster's Dictionary defines *discipline* as "training that develops self-control, character, or efficiency. The results of such training; orderly conduct. Submission to authority and control. Treatment that corrects or punishes."

The apostle Paul said that *"every man that striveth for the mastery is temperate in all things"* (I Corinthians 9:25). Do you want self-control (one of the fruit of the Spirit), character, and efficiency in your life? Do you want your life to have order? Do you want the blessings of God that come through submission to authority and self-control? If you answered *yes* to these questions, then you need self-discipline to be an integral part of your life!

HOW TO START
    I. Wake up to your need for self-discipline. Set a goal

of disciplining yourself to become obedient to God. Ask God to disturb you and wake you up anytime.

2. Realize there are no shortcuts.

3. Pray every day for the desire to be self-disciplined in every area of your life (name them).

4. Receive your motivation from Jesus.

5. Start with small daily chores such as flossing your teeth, making your bed, putting away things (iron, mail, shoes, etc.). Add one or two spiritual disciplines such as reading your Bible at the same time daily, fasting the same day every week, praying at the same time every day. Small disciplines will help you to accomplish great things in life. They will also help you to stand in the face of adversity. Daniel did not bow to a decree against him and his God in his latter years because he did not bow by eating the king's meat in his younger years.

It takes twenty-one to thirty days to create true discipline. If you fall short, start again wherever you left off.

Self-discipline is a muscle;
you must choose to exercise it!

Prayer Aid

Jesus, please forgive me for my lack of self-discipline. I have allowed the small foxes to spoil the vine by my lack of discipline. Lord, help me to discipline my life to Your Word and to Your Spirit. Put within my heart a goal. Grant me the grace I need to consistently put forth the effort to reach my goal.

Lord, I realize there are no shortcuts, and all I need is an obedient and willing heart. Grant me the ability to perform what You have put in my heart. For it is written, "*Now therefore perform the doing of it; that as there was a readiness to will, so there may be a performance also out of that which ye have. For if there be first a willing mind, it is accepted according to that a man hath, and not according to that he hath not*" (II Corinthians 8:11-12).

Chapter Five

CONSECRATION

For the law maketh men high priests which have infirmity;
but the word of the oath, which was since the law, maketh the Son,
who is consecrated for evermore.

HEBREWS 7:28

Consecration

Consecration sets the course of your life in Christ Jesus. Prayer is the inlet and the outlet of a consecrated life. Prayer can influence your level of consecration, and consecration definitely influences your level of prayer.

Webster's defines *consecration* as "to set apart as holy; devote to religious use; make or declare sacred. To devote, dedicate, to cause to be revered or honored."

The definition for the word *consecrate* in Hebrew is derived from combining two words: the first word is *malay*. It means "to fill, be full of, accomplish, confirm and consecrate, be at an end, fulfill, flow, furnish, gather, presume, replenish, satisfy." The second word is *yad,* which means "a hand (the open one, indicating power, means, direction), to be able." In summary, when you come to the end of yourself and become completely full of God, you will accomplish and fulfill His will for your life. Your consecration will manifest His power, means, and direction in your life.

The Greek definition for *consecration* also consists of two words: The first word is *teleioo.* It means "to complete, accomplish, or consummate (in character); consecrate, finish, fulfill, make perfect." The root word of *teleioo* is *telos.* *Telos* means "to set out for a definite point or goal; the point aimed at as a limit; the conclusion of an act or state; result (ultimate or prophetic), purpose." The second word is *egkainia* which means "to renew, inaugurate, consecrate, and dedicate."

Consecration is the means by which you reach your eternal goal: ruling and reigning with Jesus forever! *"He that endureth to the end shall be saved"* (Matthew 10:22).

Our entire walk with God is to bring us to an expected end. Jeremiah 29:11 says, *"For I know the thoughts that I think toward you, saith the LORD, thoughts of peace, and not of evil, to give you an expected end [or an end and expectation]."*

We are in a race. We are living in the most exciting and treacherous time known to man. Could it be that the last baton in the Gentile age has been passed to this generation of Apostolics? When running a relay race, you use your best runners at the beginning and at the end of the race. Could it be that God desires to manifest the kingdom of God in all of its power and glory through us?

Oftentimes, we do not consider the end of a matter; we live for the here and now. A consecrated life looks both at the present and into the future. The apostle Paul said to Timothy, *"I have fought a good fight, I have finished my course, I have kept the faith: henceforth there is laid up for me a crown of righteousness, which the Lord, the righteous judge, shall give me at that day: and not to me only, but unto all them also that love his appearing"* (II Timothy 4:7-8).

Hebrews 12:1-2 sheds further light on consecration: *"Wherefore seeing we also are compassed about with so great a cloud of witnesses, let us lay aside **every** weight, and the sin which doth so easily beset us, and let us run with patience the race that is set before us. Looking unto Jesus the author and finisher of our faith; who for the joy that was set before him endured the cross, despising the shame, and is set down at the right hand of the throne of God."*

When you are consecrated to the Lord, you are set apart for Him and His purposes. You are complete and full in Him. The end of your expectation is in Him!

Jesus lived a consecrated life before His disciples and expected them to do the same. We are His disciples today, and we, too, must live consecrated lives before Him.

To live a consecrated life, our hearts cannot be divided between God and the world. One of the definitions of the word world in Greek (from *cosmos*) means "adorning." We must lay aside the adorning of this world for the adorning of Christ Jesus. We must become single-minded in the cause of Christ. Therefore let us take inventory of our hearts and consecrate our lives afresh to the Lord!

Prayer Aid

To help you further develop a consecrated life, pray and meditate on the following scriptures. These Scriptures give insight into what God expects to see in a consecrated life:

Enter ye in at the strait gate: for wide is the gate,
and broad is the way, that leadeth to destruction, and many there be
which go in thereat: because strait is the gate, and narrow is the way,
which leadeth unto life, and few there be that find it.
MATTHEW 7:13-14

If any man will come after me, let him deny himself,
and take up his cross, and follow me. For whosoever will save
his life shall lose it: and whosoever will lose his life
for my sake shall find it.
MATTHEW 16:24-25

The light of the body is the eye: therefore when thine eye is single,
thy whole body also is full of light; but when thine eye is evil,
thy body also is full of darkness.
LUKE 11:34

Labour not for the meat which perisheth, but for that meat which
endureth unto everlasting life, which the Son of man shall give
unto you: for him hath God the Father sealed.
JOHN 6:27

I beseech you therefore, brethren, by the mercies of God,
that ye present your bodies a living sacrifice, holy, acceptable

unto God, which is your reasonable service. And be not conformed
to this world: but be ye transformed by the renewing of your mind,
that ye may prove what is that good, and acceptable,
and perfect, will of God.

ROMANS 12:1-2

Wherefore come out from among them, and be ye separate,
saith the Lord, and touch not the unclean thing;
and I will receive you.

II CORINTHIANS 6:17

For the grace of God that bringeth salvation hath appeared
to all men, teaching us that, denying ungodliness and worldly lusts,
we should live soberly, righteously, and godly, in this present world.

TITUS 2:11-12

Pure religion and undefiled before God and the Father is this,
to visit the fatherless and widows in their affliction,
and to keep himself unspotted from the world.

JAMES 1:27

Love not the world, neither the things that are in the world.
If any man love the world, the love of the Father is not in him.
For all that is in the world, the lust of the flesh, and the lust of the eyes,
and the pride of life, is not of the Father, but is of the world.
And the world passeth away, and the lust thereof: but he
that doeth the will of God abideth for ever.

I JOHN 2:15-17

For whatsoever is born of God overcometh the world:
and this is the victory that overcometh the world, even our faith.
I JOHN 5:4

No man that warreth entangleth himself with the affairs of this life;
that he may please him who hath chosen him to be a soldier.
II TIMOTHY 2:4

Chapter Six

ENTERING IN

*Enter into his gates with thanksgiving, and into his courts
with praise: be thankful unto him, and bless his name.*

PSALM 100:4

Thanksgiving

Why do we enter into His gates with thanksgiving? What does it mean to enter into His gates?

In the Hebrew, the word *gates* is *shahar*. It means "an opening; for example, a door or gate of a city." The word *shahar* has its origin in the word *shawar,* which means "to split or open," for example, to act as gatekeeper. It also means "to estimate or think."

Could it be that our thoughts, when directed toward Him, cause the gates of His tabernacle or "His heart" to open? Could it be that when we are entering into His gates, we are entering into His thoughts? Could it be that thanksgiving is the best way to redirect our thinking toward Him?

When we begin to thank Him for the small things and the great things, we begin to recognize Jesus as the source of our substance as well as our existence. Have you ever received a thank-you card you really appreciated? We all like to be thanked for acts of kindness. How much more should the Lord be thanked, for He *"daily loadeth us with benefits"* (Psalm 68:19).

When we enter into His gates with thanksgiving, we are cultivating a thankful heart. II Timothy 3:2 tells us that in the last days men will be unthankful. Unthankfulness has its roots in bitterness and rebellion. What better way to shake off this end-time attitude than by giving thanks in all things! I Thessalonians 5:18 says, *"In every thing give thanks: for this is the will of God in Christ Jesus concerning you."*

Praise

Praise is the outward manifestation of a pure and thankful heart. *Halal* is the Hebrew word that means "praise." It means "to be clear; to shine; hence to make a show, to boast; and thus to be clamorously foolish; to rave; to celebrate; also to stultify." *Stultify* means "to cause to appear foolish, stupid, inconsistent, etc.; make absurd or ridiculous. To cause to be of no effect; make worthless or useless: as, his present behavior stultifies his previous efforts."

Why would God desire and applaud such praise from His creation? First we must recognize that God's thoughts are not our thoughts and His ways are not our ways (Isaiah 55:8-9). I Corinthians 1:18-29 reveals God's heart regarding wisdom and foolishness. Verses 27-29 read, *"But God hath chosen the foolish things of the world to confound the wise; and God hath chosen the weak things of the world to confound the things which are mighty; and base things of the world, and things which are despised, hath God chosen, yea, and things which are not, to bring to nought things that are: that no flesh should glory in his presence."*

Praise that appears foolish and clamorous to men is glorious to God because He is receiving all the glory!

Reverend Teklemariam from Ethiopia and several other ministers were about to be killed for the name of Jesus. While surrounded by men with broken bottles and other various types of weapons, they began to praise the Lord clamorously. The result was God's judgment. The man who was about to give the death orders had a sudden heart attack. The fear of God came over the other men and many were saved.

"Rejoice in the LORD, O ye righteous: for praise is comely for the upright. Praise God in his sanctuary: praise him in the firmament of his power. Praise him for his mighty acts: praise him according to his excellent greatness. Praise him with the sound of the trumpet: praise him with the psaltery and harp. Praise him with the timbrel and dance: praise him with stringed instruments and organs. Praise him upon the loud cymbals: praise him upon the high sounding cymbals. Let every thing that hath breath praise the LORD. Praise ye the LORD" (Psalm 33:1; 150:1-6).

Worship

Revelations 22:8-9 says, *"And I John saw these things, and heard them. And when I had heard and seen, I fell down to worship before the feet of the angel which shewed me these things. Then saith he unto me, See thou do it not: for I am thy fellowservant, and of thy brethren the prophets, and of them which keep the sayings of this book: Worship God."*

It is within the nature of man to worship. What he worships is determined by the state of his heart. We find in the above passage that worship belongs to God—anything or anyone else we worship is an idol. Jesus Himself said to Satan, *"Thou shalt worship the Lord thy God, and him only shalt thou serve"* (Matthew 4:10).

It is not difficult to find out what a man worships, because out of the abundance of the heart the mouth speaks. What's in the heart of a man will appear within a short time during a conversation. If a man worships God, he will talk about God. If a man worships cars, he will talk about cars. If a man worships sports, he will talk about sports. If a man worships food, he will center his conversation on food. To reiterate, worship of anyone or anything other than God is idolatry. It was idolatry that caused Israel to fall away from God again and again and to experience the judgment of God's hand against them.

Worship belongs to God. It is a holy act of bowing or making yourself prostrate in homage to the royalty of God. It is accompanied with an attitude of humility, honor, and reverence. When true worship overtakes our hearts, we will find ourselves desiring to decrease that He may increase. It is in this state that we begin to recognize our sinful nature and insignificance in comparison to His significance and glory. It was Isaiah who saw the Lord sitting on a throne, high and lifted up, with His train filling the Temple. He heard one seraph cry to another, saying, *"Holy, holy, holy, is the* LORD *of hosts: the whole earth is full of his glory"* (Isaiah 6:3). And the posts of the door moved at the voice of him that cried, and the house was filled with smoke. Then Isaiah cried, *"Woe is me! for I am undone; because I am a man of unclean lips . . . for mine eyes have seen the King, the* LORD *of hosts"* (Isaiah 6:5).

Worship also denotes a motion toward, accession to, or nearness at. It is drawing near to God with a humble heart that will automatically lead us into repentance.

Chapter Seven

REPENTANCE

And Jesus answering said unto them, Suppose ye that these Galilaeans
were sinners above all the Galilaeans, because they suffered such things?
I tell you, Nay: but, except ye repent, ye shall all likewise perish.

LUKE 13:2-3

"Every sin consists of the deed and of the attitudes that underlie it. Just as man can more easily control his hands than his eyes, his actions than his imagination, so it is infinitely easier to avoid sinning in deed and to repent from sinful deeds than it is to avoid, and repent from, sinful thoughts" (Shaarei Teshuva 3:26, Talmud).

"For the wages of sin is death; but the gift of God is eternal life through Jesus Christ our Lord" (Romans 6:23). The Bible teaches us that death reigned from Adam to Moses even though there was no law until Moses. Moreover, it was through one man's disobedience that many were made sinners and through one man's (Jesus Christ) obedience that

many are made righteous.

Repentance is a life and death issue. It is indicative of dying to our sinful nature and turning toward God. If we choose to turn away from sin and toward God through repentance, we choose life; but if we choose not to repent of our sins, then we choose death.

There is a life-giving principle that operates through death. You will notice that the life of a seed does not exist in its outer shell. But, because the outer shell is dead, when it is buried the life within that shell is quickened. All seeds must go through the death and burial process before life can spring forth. It is the outer shell that dies, allowing the life from within to come forth. Similarly, if we allow our outer man to die through repentance and then bury him in a watery grave (baptism in Jesus' name) and then receive the baptism of the Holy Spirit, then our inner man will be regenerated, and the new man will spring forth. By faith, we put off the old man (earthly nature) and put on the new man (heavenly nature), which is made after the image of Jesus Christ.

Paul gave this explanation: *"Thou fool, that which thou sowest is not quickened, except it die"* (I Corinthians 15:36). He further said, *"For if we have been planted together in the likeness of his death [water baptism], we shall also be in the likeness of his resurrection: knowing this, that our old man is crucified with him, that the body of sin might be destroyed, that henceforth we should not serve sin. For he that is dead is freed from sin"* (Romans 6:5-7).

The Scriptures further admonish us to *"let not sin there-*

fore reign in your mortal body, that ye should obey it in the lusts thereof. Neither yield ye your members as instruments of unrighteousness unto sin: but yield yourselves unto God, as those that are alive from the dead, and your members as instruments of righteousness unto God. For sin shall not have dominion over you: for ye are not under the law, but under grace" (Romans 6:12-14).

The apostle John further clarifies the position of sin in our lives: *"But if we walk in the light, as he is in the light, we have fellowship one with another, and the blood of Jesus Christ his Son cleanseth us from all sin. . . . If we confess our sins, he is faithful and just to forgive us our sins, and to cleanse us from all unrighteousness. . . . My little children, these things I write unto you, that ye sin not. And if any man sin, we have an advocate with the Father, Jesus Christ the righteous: and he is the propitiation for our sins: and not for ours only, but also for the sins of the whole world"* (1 John 1:7, 9; 2:1-2).

As sinners, we repent of our sins as the first step toward regeneration (newness of life), and as saints, we repent of our sins in the ongoing process of sanctification (purification). In either case, true repentance will always produce fruit or good works that confirm it has taken place. A person who repents but still continues to commit the same sin is still struggling with an aspect of his old fleshly nature.

In Hebrew, the word *repentance* means "to sigh, as in breathing strongly; to be sorry, to give an answer." In Greek, *repentance* means "compunction (to prick or sting; a poignant uneasiness proceeding from a sense of guilt of consciousness causing pain; the sting of conscience; pricking of heart:

remorse), to think differently, change direction, reforma-
tion, reversal of (another's) decision." It is through repentance that a person turns back to God.

Jesus Christ took upon Himself all of our sins: *"For
he hath made him to be sin for us, who knew no sin; that we might be
made the righteousness of God in him"* (II Corinthians 5:21). He
who knew no sin became sin for us. This includes past, present, and future sins. He bore the punishment not only for
our sinful acts but also for our sinful attitudes. He also
bore the emotions caused by sin, grief, and sorrow. In addition, He took upon Himself the curses that sin brought
into the world. One such curse is sickness, another such
curse is death. The wrath of God was poured out on Jesus
so that we might escape the judgment and wrath of God
appointed to all people. All of this culminated on a cross
set on a hill called Calvary.

The people were pricked in their hearts upon hearing
the words of the apostle Peter, *"Therefore let all the house of
Israel know assuredly, that God hath made that same Jesus, whom ye
have crucified, both Lord and Christ."* Likewise, we must be
pricked in our hearts when we realize that He died at
Calvary for our sins. Our conscience will lead us to
repentance. Repentance is the first step to being born
again.

We become regenerated and begin the process of
sanctification when we are born again of water and Spirit.
When we believe and obey the gospel ("Repent, and be
baptized every one of you in the name of Jesus Christ for

the remission of sins, and ye shall receive the gift of the Holy Ghost" [Acts 2:38]), we become regenerated through the atoning work that Jesus Christ wrought at Calvary. Although we are set free from the bondage of sin and regenerated unto newness of life, our outer man, or our sin nature, attempts to resurrect itself in our lives (Romans 7:14-25). Nevertheless, our inner man (our regenerated spirit) has the power through "putting on Christ" to mortify the deeds of the flesh (Romans 8:13; Galatians 3:27; Colossians 3:5).

The Word teaches us that sanctification is the process by which God purifies us. Although we have received our purification by faith, we must manifest what we have received by obeying God's Word through the Spirit we have received. I Peter 1:22 says, *"Seeing ye have purified your souls in obeying the truth through the Spirit unto unfeigned love of the brethren, see that ye love one another . . . fervently."* And I John 3:3 says, *"And every man that hath this hope in him purifieth himself, even as he is pure."*

The purification of our lives first begins at the new birth and continues as we recognize attitudes, actions, expressions, and thoughts in our lives that are contrary to the teachings of the Word of God. In addition, purification comes through learning who we are in Christ and walking in that knowledge (Hosea 4:6; Ephesians 4:21-24; I John 3:9). Any pattern in our lives that does not line up with the Word of God is sin! Sin simply means to miss the mark. Iniquity is sin we are intentionally hiding in our hearts.

When we recognize sin in our lives, we must make confession and forsake that sin. As long as we remain impenitent over sin in our lives, we are not in right standing with God. Proverbs 28:13 says, *"He that covereth his sins shall not prosper: but whoso confesseth and forsaketh them shall have mercy."* I John 1:9-10 says, *"If we confess our sins, he is faithful and just to forgive us our sins, and to cleanse us from all unrighteousness. If we say that we have not sinned, we make him a liar, and his word is not in us."*

If our sin has caused a problem with another individual, we also must, if possible, make confession to that individual and make any restitution necessary. James 5:16 says, *"Confess your faults one to another, and pray one for another, that ye may be healed. The effectual fervent prayer of a righteous man availeth much."* Confession is not just saying we're sorry. We must name and forsake the sin and the root of it to receive true deliverance from it.

Confession places us in right standing with God because it releases God to forgive and cleanse us with His blood. This act restores us to right relationship with God. A person who is in right standing with God is righteous in the eyes of God, and his prayers avail much.

Once our sins have been confessed, we need to replant the garden of our heart with the Word of God. Herein lies a principle seen in every area of life: We reap what we sow. The Word is "seed" and needs to be planted into the soil of our hearts. If it is watered with prayer and faith, over time we will begin to see signs of growth and eventually fruit from that seed (Word). If we engraft Scriptures on temperance into our souls, one day we will *automatically* see temperance become a part of our actions and thoughts.

James 1:21 says, *"Wherefore lay apart all filthiness and super-fluity of naughtiness, and receive with meekness the engrafted word, which is able to save your souls."*

The following is a short compilation of sins that are confessed on the day of Yom Kippur, the Day of Atonement. Yom Kippur is observed by the Jewish community around the world, and the entire day is spent in corporate repentance. Let us prayerfully consider what we are about to read. A little leaven leavens the whole lump. Remember we must first remove the beam from our own eye before we try to help remove the speck in our brother or sister's eye. Satan is an accuser of the brethren; God is a forgiver of the brethren. If we are ever going to experience the freedom to live a righteous and holy life before God and man, we must see the sin that is blinding and binding our lives.

The following is based on the book *Viduy* by Rabbi Nosson Scherman:

For the sin that we have sinned against You . . .

We are chagrined (deeply sorrowful, embarrassed, mortified) and humiliated because we have acted against Your will. We are doubly ashamed when we consider how lowly we are and how exalted You are. How could we have dared sin against you!

Under duress and willingly

We have said we had no choice but to sin; and we sinned willingly because we could not resist temptation.

Under duress: Often we sin because we put ourselves into a predicament where we rationalize that we have no choice but to sin. For example, if we are afraid we may lose our jobs or customers, we may permit ourselves to do things that we know to be wrong and would not condone in others.

Willingly: We have sinned simply because we wanted to indulge a pleasure. How often have we condoned a misdeed simply because we wanted to please someone or to enjoy an experience! Such desire is one of the main causes of sin.

Through hardness of the heart

We have refused to admit we might be wrong. We have had the attitude of "I am always right!" Such arrogance gives birth to stubbornness, refusing to admit our shortcomings, and to a lack of compassion for the needs of the poor and the infirm. God gave us a free will so that we could make intelligent choices, not so that we should refuse to see the truth.

Without knowledge

We have sinned through ignorance. We have failed to think carefully or learn enough. Failure to study the Bible leads inevitably to sin, and lack of insight or information causes people to misjudge situations. Remember self-imposed ignorance is no excuse.

With the utterance of the lips

We were too quick to promise or speak. We have uttered vows and oaths, although we have been taught that it is best to avoid such utterances, even if they will be kept secret. We have expressed ourselves harshly against our fellows, hurting or shaming them. And when we were dissatisfied with events, we even expressed complaints against God.

We have sinned because of hasty promises. We have made promises that we could not possibly keep. And we have made rash statements and then felt compelled to justify them or to act upon them.

In public or in private

Sometimes we meant to be noticed; sometimes we thought no one would know.

In public: A public sin is serious not only because of the act but also because it can desecrate God's name in the eyes of onlookers. We may do foolish or sinful things to attract attention and approval.

In private: A private sin, on the other hand, is contemptible because the perpetrator seems to fear human disapproval more than God's anger. We have reassured ourselves that if no one sees, we are free to sin.

The following confessions have been compiled by the author of this book:

Lord, we have sinned against You . . .
We have become lovers of our own selves

Our actions and motives have been selfish, and we have failed to care about the things of God and of others as we should. Galatians 5:13-15 says, *"For, brethren, ye have been called unto liberty; only use not liberty for an occasion to the flesh, but by love serve one another. For all the law is fulfilled in one word, even in this; Thou shalt love thy neighbour as thyself. But if ye bite and devour one another, take heed that ye be not consumed one of another."* Philippians 2:3-5 states, *"Let nothing be done through strife or vainglory; but in lowliness of mind let each esteem other better than themselves. Look not every man on his own things, but every man also on the things of others. Let this mind be in you, which was also in Christ Jesus."*

We have entertained covetousness

We have become greedy and lusted after the possessions of others and of this world. I John 2:15-17 says, *"Love not the world, neither the things that are in the world. If any man love the world, the love of the Father is not in him. For all that is in the world, the lust of the flesh, and the lust of the eyes, and the pride of life, is not of the Father, but is of the world. And the world passeth away, and the lust thereof: but he that doeth the will of God abideth for ever."*

We have become boasters

We boast in our hearts and with others of our worldly and spiritual accomplishments. I Corinthians 13:4 says, *"Charity suffereth long, and is kind; charity envieth not; charity vaunteth not itself, is not puffed up."* (The word *vaunteth* means "to boast.")

We have become proud
We have failed to humble ourselves before God and one another. We have maintained our own views with arrogance, even to the destruction of unity among our fellow family members and the body of Jesus Christ. We think our own way is the best way, without considering or submitting to the ideas and ways of others. We have desired control over our own lives and the lives of others. Proverbs 13:10 counsels, *"Only by pride cometh contention: but with the well advised is wisdom."* Ezekiel 16:49 warns, *"Behold, this was the iniquity of thy sister Sodom, pride, fulness of bread, and abundance of idleness was in her and in her daughters, neither did she strengthen the hand of the poor and needy."*

We have failed to submit to authority
We have failed to submit to church, governmental, parental, and secular authority. We have even mocked authority and have spoken evil of dignitaries out of a proud and rebellious heart. We have failed to comply with the Word of God regarding submission and have helped to breed disrespect and rebellion in our church and society. Hebrews 13:17 says, *"Obey them that have the rule over you, and submit yourselves: for they watch for your souls, as they that must give account, that they may do it with joy, and not with grief: for that is unprofitable for you."*
I Peter 2:13-15, 18 states, *"Submit yourselves to every ordinance of man for the Lord's sake: whether it be to the king, as supreme; or unto governors, as unto them that are sent by him for the punishment*

of evildoers, and for the praise of them that do well. For so is the will of God, that with well doing ye may put to silence the ignorance of foolish men. . . . Servants, be subject to your masters with all fear; not only to the good and gentle, but also to the froward."

We have been guilty of gossip and slander

We have caused discord in our homes, on our jobs, and among our brothers and sisters by spreading gossip and speaking slander. We have spoken words that can damage the credibility and character of another, whether they have been true or false. We have not gone to our brother or sister privately to take care of our offenses or to reprove him or her of sin. Therefore we have harbored bitterness, unforgiveness, and resentment in our hearts toward one another. We must not allow unforgiveness, which leads to bitterness, to remain in our hearts since it is a root of gossip and slander. Matthew 18:15 declares, *"Moreover if thy brother shall trespass against thee, go and tell him his fault between thee and him alone: if he shall hear thee, thou hast gained thy brother."*

We have become lovers of pleasures, more than lovers of God

We have given ourselves to fleshly desires and failed to abstain from fleshly lusts which war against our souls. We have failed to take up our cross and follow You by denying ourselves and taking on the cause of Your kingdom. We have been idle in the things of God. We have allowed our minds to become idle by indulging ourselves in worldly entertainment, such as television programs, talk shows,

videos, video games, and sports. We have desired to fellowship more than to pray, to eat more than to fast, to play
more than to study the Word, and to be entertained more
than to reach the lost. Lord, forgive us for not giving ourselves to Your purpose and cause through prayer, fasting,
the study of Your Word, and evangelism. Help us, Lord, to
return to You with all of our heart, soul, mind, and
strength. Help us to shun worldliness and desire godliness
and holiness.

James 1:27 says, *"Pure religion and undefiled before God and
the Father is this, to visit the fatherless and widows in their affliction,
and to keep himself unspotted from the world."*

We have failed to recognize the need to repent for others

It is not enough to repent for ourselves. Throughout
the Scriptures, we read the accounts of men who continu-
ally were repenting for their people and for their nation. It
is important to repent for the sins of our ancestors, for
others, and for our nation, asking God to be merciful.
Daniel stood in the gap for his people when he began to
seek the Lord God through prayer and fasting.

Daniel 9:4-6 says, *"And I prayed unto the LORD my God,
and made my confession, and said, O Lord, the great and dreadful
God, keeping the covenant and mercy to them that love him, and to
them that keep his commandments; we have sinned, and have committed iniquity, and have done wickedly, and have rebelled, even by departing from thy precepts and from thy judgments: neither have we heark-
ened unto thy servants the prophets, which spake in thy name to our*

kings, our princes, and our fathers, and to all the people of the land." (Continue to pray the ninth chapter of Daniel through verse 19.)

You may have felt a conviction or a quickened awareness of sin in your life while reading the above confessions; please take a moment to confess the sins that were revealed to you. You can confess and renounce your sins with assurance of forgiveness: *"If we confess our sins, he is faithful and just to forgive us our sins, and to cleanse us from all unrighteousness"* (1 John 1:9).

What is the Difference Between Conviction and Condemnation

Conviction leaves after sincere repentance; condemnation stays. Conviction leaves because we have confidence that God has heard our prayer and has forgiven our sins. If our heart condemns us, God is greater than our heart, and knows all things. It is important to know the truth in every situation. Any feeling or thought that does not line up with the Word of God is a lie and can bring you into condemnation. Ask God to reveal the truth to you and then confess it. You will receive an instant release. For example, if you feel condemnation after sincerely repenting, meditate and speak aloud 1 John 1:9. You can also say, "I bind the spirit of condemnation and guilt. I have been forgiven and cleansed from all unrighteousness through His blood. Therefore, I stand in the righteousness of Jesus Christ, who has destroyed the works of Satan and has overcome the world."

Conclusion

Let us guard our hearts with all diligence through repentance. God judges sin in our lives, and if we will learn to judge ourselves, we will not be judged. I Corinthians 11:29-32 teaches us that if we allow sin to go unconfessed, we are not discerning the body of Jesus Christ. In other words, we are not recognizing and accepting His finished work of Calvary. The Scripture continues to tell us that because of this many are weak, sickly, or have died. Paul states that the antidote is judging ourselves: *"For if we would judge ourselves, we should not be judged. But when we are judged, we are chastened of the Lord, that we should not be condemned with the world."*

Oftentimes, we fail to consider that weakness, sickness, or severe fatigue can result from unrepented sin in our lives. This unrepented sin brings God's chastisement to reveal the sin in order for repentance to take place.

As you can see, repentance is needful not only when we first come to God, but also in our daily living. II Corinthians 7:10 says, *"For godly sorrow worketh repentance to salvation not to be repented of [turned away from]: but the sorrow of the world worketh death."*

Chapter Eight

PETITION

Be careful for nothing; but in every thing by prayer and supplication
wtih thanksgiving let your requests be made known unto God.
PHILIPPIANS 4:6

Petition is humbly and earnestly making our requests known to God. It is unloading all of our cares and burdens into the hands of the Lord and trusting Him to answer our petitions. It is not enough for us to petition God for our earthly needs, but we also must petition God for our spiritual needs. You can pray the Word of God into your situation. We must learn not to focus on the problem but to find the solution to the problem in the Word of God!

For example, if you are consumed with the cares of this life, such as food, clothes, bills, and so on, meditate on and pray Matthew 6:25: "*Therefore I say unto you, Take no thought for your life, what ye shall eat, or what ye shall drink; nor yet for your body, what ye shall put on. Is not the life more than meat, and the body than raiment?"*

If you are double-minded and have difficulty keeping your word, meditate, memorize, and pray Matthew 5:37: *"But let your communication be Yea, yea; Nay, nay: for whatsoever is more than these cometh of evil."*

If you are having problems believing God will answer your petitions, meditate and pray Mark 11:24: *"Therefore I say unto you, What things soever ye desire, when ye pray, believe that ye receive them, and ye shall have them."*

We can make humble petition to God according to: **Our needs:** *"Have mercy upon me, O LORD, for I am in trouble: mine eye is consumed with grief, yea, my soul and my belly"* (Psalm 31:9); **The promises of God:** *"And thou saidst, I will surely do thee good, and make thy seed as the sand of the sea, which cannot be numbered for multitude"* (Genesis 32:12); **God's mercy:** *"O my God, incline thine ear, and hear; open thine eyes, and behold our desolations, and the city which is called by thy name: for we do not present our supplications before thee for our righteousnesses, but for thy great mercies"* (Daniel 9:18); **God's glory:** *"And say ye, Save us, O God of our salvation, and gather us together, and deliver us from the heathen, that we may give thanks to thy holy name, and glory in thy praise"* (I Chronicles 16:35); **God's justice:** *"And Abraham drew near, and said, Wilt thou also destroy the righteous with the wicked?"* (Genesis 18:23); **Your faith in God:** *"O keep my soul, and deliver me: let me not be ashamed; for I put my trust in thee"* (Psalm 25:20); **Your past good works:** *"Think upon me, my God, for good, according to all that I have done for this people"* (Nehemiah 5:19); **Your good works to come:** *"I will run the way of thy* *commandments, when thou shalt enlarge my heart"* (Psalm 119:32).

Petitioning the Lord for our needs teaches us to lean on the Lord and not on our own flesh. It is an act of humility. It daily brings to the forefront the source of our blessings, provision, and strength. Even in our times of prosperity, we must always remember that Jesus—and not the work of our own hands—is our source: *"Cursed be the man that trusteth in man, and maketh flesh his arm, and whose heart departeth from the* LORD. . . . *Blessed is the man that trusteth in the* LORD, *and whose hope the* LORD *is"* (Jeremiah 17:5, 7).

Never feel that any petition you may have is too small or too big. I often hear people say, "That is just a small thing; I am not going to bother God with that." That type of thinking needs to be changed in us. If it's the small foxes that spoil the vine, then it may be that we need to bring the little things before God so that they do not become big things. The Lord says we are to be careful for nothing but in everything make our requests known to Him. In other words, ask . . . ask . . . ask.

God does not answer a petition according to its measure of importance or size, but He answers it according to our faith, His will, and the motive of our heart. James 4:3 says, *"Ye ask, and receive not, because ye ask amiss, that ye may consume it upon your lusts."* If you are sensitive to the Spirit of God, you will have an immediate sense whether or not what you are asking is in alignment with God's will. Oftentimes, when you are making a petition that is not in agreement with God's will, you will feel either a check or prompting in your heart that lets you know you are asking wrongly.

"But seek ye first the kingdom of God, and His righteousness; and all these things shall be added unto you" (Matthew 6:33).

Prayer Aid

Lord, I come before You today not only for my natural needs but also for my spiritual needs. The things that are temporal will pass away, but he that does the will of God will abide forever. Lord, equip me this day to do Your will. Help me to add those things to my life that will glorify You and subtract those things from my life that will bring reproach to You and Your kingdom. Lord, grant me this day a fervent desire for Your word, prayer, fasting, and evangelism. Help me to live a consecrated and holy life. Help me to lean upon Your righteousness which is by faith and not to establish my own righteousness. Renew my mind that I may prove what is Your acceptable will for my life. As I walk through this day, cause me to be sensitive to the needs of others. Let Your burden and compassion for the lost burn within my heart. Help me to lay aside my own agenda and follow the leading of Your Spirit and Word. Grant me boldness to witness to those around me. Help me not to think upon my own issues but upon the issues of others. Lead me not into temptation, but deliver me from evil. Lord, I pray the whole armor of God upon myself, my family, and my friends. Cause me to recognize the wiles of the devil and resist him steadfast in the faith. Lord, do not allow Satan to impose his will on my life and the lives of those I love. Amen.

Chapter Nine

SUPPLICATION: CRY OF THE HOUR

*I exhort therefore, that, first of all, supplications, prayers,
intercessions, and giving of thanks, be made for all men;
for kings, and for all that are in authority; that we may lead
a quiet and peaceable life in all godliness and honesty.
For this is good and acceptable in the sight of God our Saviour;
who will have all men to be saved, and to come
unto the knowledge of the truth.*

1 TIMOTHY 2:1-4

Supplication Prayer

Supplication prayer is prayer that moves the heart of
God in such a way that it causes the favor of God to
rest on the person and his petition.

The Hebrew word translated *supplication* is the same
word used for *grace*. Grace is the unmerited favor or divine
assistance of God in a person's life. Supplication is an
action that brings God's favor into a particular petition. It
is not just bringing your petition before God; it is the

manner and attitude by which you bring your petition before God.

In the Old Testament, those who feared God understood that everything came from God, good or bad. They understood that whatever was happening to them God had allowed. Therefore, they turned to God in the time of need. They rent their clothes, put on sackcloth and ashes, humbled their hearts, and sought the Lord for an answer, a direction, and deliverance. On the contrary, those who did not seek God for help, but who went down into Egypt for their help, were destroyed.

Supplication is bringing your petition humbly before the Lord. It is often characterized by weeping and confession of sin. It is entreating the Lord with brokenness and contrition for a particular situation. It can include heart-wrenching prayer. It is oftentimes accompanied with fasting, even to the degree of complete abstinence from food and water. It is serious prayer.

Supplication prayer is the type of prayer that should be used when presenting a case to the Lord. Daniel's intercession for the nation of Israel is an excellent model for true supplication. Read Daniel 9:1-21. Daniel's reading of the Book of Jeremiah prompted his intercession for Israel. In particular, Jeremiah's prophecies concerning the destruction and desolation of Jerusalem rang in Daniel's ears and stirred him to supplicate God for Israel. (See Jeremiah 4:1-9, 14-15, 19-22, 28, 30-31 for examples of what Daniel pondered.) Daniel was just a boy when Jeremiah proclaimed judgment upon Israel. During his latter years in Babylon, the more he studied and pondered the words of Jeremiah, the more the cry for repentance stirred his heart. Daniel could have asked himself, "Why didn't we listen to the prophet? Why didn't we heed his words? Why didn't we humble ourselves and turn toward our God? Why didn't we obey His voice?"

Jeremiah's words pierced Daniel's heart, and a cry came from his innermost being, "Lord, have we not suffered long enough? Will You not build us again, and take away our captivity? When, O God, will You deliver us, when? Lord, as suddenly as You brought destruction, that is how suddenly You can restore us if we turn back to You."

Through tears that flowed like a river down his face, Daniel sought an answer from his God. He searched the Scriptures chapter after chapter, line after line, word after word to understand and to know the times, the seasons, and the end of his people. As he wiped the tears away from his eyes and blotted them off the pages of the ancient manuscripts, he began to feel the heartbeat of God stirring his soul.

A feeling of hope came alive in Daniel's soul when he came to a particular prophecy of Jeremiah regarding the restoration of his people. Jeremiah 29:10-14 says, *"For thus saith the LORD, That after seventy years be accomplished at Babylon I will visit you, and perform my good word toward you, in causing you to return to this place. For I know the thoughts that I think toward you, saith the LORD, thoughts of peace, and not of evil, to give you an expected end. Then shall ye call upon me, and ye shall go and pray unto me, and I will hearken unto you. And ye shall seek me, and find me, when ye shall search for me with all your heart. And I will be found of you, saith the LORD: and I will turn away your captivity, and I will gather you from all the nations, and from all the places whither I have driven you, saith the LORD; and I will bring you again into the place whence I caused you to be carried away captive."*

Daniel began to seek out the days that he and his people had been in captivity. He counted the years and understood that the days of their captivity would soon come to an end. It is with this understanding and in this setting that Daniel set his face toward the Lord God, to seek Him through prayer and supplication, with fasting and sackcloth and ashes, for the restoration of his people and of his land.

Read Daniel 9:3-19 for the supplication prayer that Daniel prayed in his humbled state before God on behalf of Israel. What a heartfelt case Daniel presented before God. He was so honest with God. His heart was humble and contrite. He explained to God the reasons why they were in captivity, and then he pleaded on their behalf for God's pardon according to His great and divine attributes of mercy and forgiveness. Daniel's supplication so moved God that He sent the angel Gabriel to speak face-to-face with Daniel (Daniel 9:21). Daniel then received understanding about the ages to come. He received understanding of God's judgment and the redemptive plan not only for his people at that time but also for these last days.

Think about it! We are living in the prophetic understanding that God revealed to Daniel for the last days. What would God do for a man or woman today that would take his church, his city, his nation to heart and make supplication on their behalf? Oh, the influence of supplication prayer!

A Look at America

"Keep, ancient lands, your stored pomp! . . .
Give me your tired, your poor, your huddled
masses yearning to breathe free, the wretched
refuse of your teeming shore. Send these,
the homeless, tempest-tossed to me.
I lift my lamp beside the golden door!"
—INSCRIPTION, STATUE OF LIBERTY

Oh, America the beautiful, home of the brave and the free. Our forefathers fought for your independence, and in 1776 you, the United States of America, emerged as a nation. They fought so you could be one nation, under God, to pursue life, liberty, and happiness. They fought for you to become a nation set apart from all nations, a Christian nation, and a nation that emulates the divine nature of God through its ethics, laws, and principles. They fought to lift up the righteous standard of a holy, omnipotent God Who rules and reigns in the heavens above and the earth beneath.

Upon the vote for the Declaration of Independence on July 4, 1776, Samuel Adams said: "We have this day

restored the sovereign to whom alone men ought to be obedient. He reigns in heaven and, from the rising to the setting sun, may his kingdom come."

For many of us today, it's not hard to remember the
"good old days." Sin was sin, and righteousness still
reigned and ruled. "In God we trust" was not just a phrase
on a coin but a state of the heart. A president was chosen
not only for his political views but for his integrity and
righteousness also. Prayer was guiding our government, our
judicial system, our educational system, our businesses, and
the lives of our families. The blessings of God flowed like
milk and honey. What happened?

Although Jeremiah spoke in a day when Israel was in its
most corrupt state, you would think Jeremiah was proph-
esying to America today. America has reached a heightened
state of perversion and immorality. Murder and violence are
rampant. Judgment has departed and truth has fallen in the
streets. Idol worship is accepted among us as "religious
freedom." Covetousness (which is idolatry) and pride have
reached an all-time high, and as the prophet said, *"From the
least of them even unto the greatest of them every one is given to covetousness; and from the prophet even unto the priest every one dealeth
falsely"* (Jeremiah 6:13). Jeremiah 18:12 says, *"And they said,
There is no hope: but we will walk after our own devices, and we will
every one do the imagination of his evil heart."*

God has removed the unseen hedges of peace and protection, which He had placed around our borders. Our
allies are becoming our enemies. We have sinned against

God and brought a terrible reproach upon His name, while still claiming to be a Christian nation. *"Be ye not deceived . . . whatsoever a man soweth, that shall he also reap"* (Galatians 6:7).

The circumstances that brought Israel to desolation and that could bring desolation to America are not much different. Yet we can learn by the past and perhaps prevent the judgment of the future. Can we change the destructive course of our nation? Can the heart of God be changed?

It is the desire of God to pour out mercy and healing into a land that returns to Him. A land that will repent of its iniquities and sins, destroy its idols, and return to the ways of God will be spared from the judgments pronounced against it. But as a nation, we must understand that the terrorizing problems we are now facing, from disease to terrorism, have been allowed by God. In other words, they are signs and manifested actions of God's judgments.

Psalm 9:17 is a very sobering Scripture: *"The wicked shall be turned into hell, and all the nations that forget God."* The only hope we have is that God's heart can still be touched through prayer and supplication. His Word still rings true: *"If my people will . . . I will"* (II Chronicles 7:14). God heard the prayers and supplications of Hezekiah, Nehemiah, Esther, and the people of Nineveh when desolation was at their door. Will He not do the same for us if we turn to Him with prayer and supplication, with fasting and weeping?

If you are reading this and you are not from the United States of America, consider your own nation. Is it in trouble

spiritually? Are the sins of your nation similar to those of
Israel? Could your nation benefit from supplication praying? Let us then turn to God with prayer and supplication
for your nation, too. Jesus is looking for *all* nations to
repent, not just Israel and America.

Zechariah 12:10 talks about the Lord pouring out a
spirit of grace and supplication upon the inhabitants of
Jerusalem, which will cause them to look upon Him Whom
they have pierced. Let us pray that God will pour out a
spirit of grace and supplication on the church today and
that we, too, may get a fresh look at Calvary for the
redemption of all mankind.

Prayer Aid

The following prayer for America and other nations is
based Daniel 9:3-19. Fill in the blanks as you are suppli-
cating for your city and nation:

"O Lord, our great and awesome God, You keep
the covenant and mercy with those who love You
and keep Your commandments. We have sinned and
have committed iniquity and have done wickedly
and have rebelled, even by departing from Your precepts and from Your judgments. We have not lis-
tened to Your servants the prophets, who have spoken in Your name to our leaders and to all the people of the land.

O Lord, righteousness belongs to You, but

open shame falls on us and on the inhabitants of
city/town and on all America/nation because of our
sins that we have committed against You. O Lord,
open shame belongs to our president, to our leaders, and to us all because we have sinned against
You. To You, Lord, belong mercy and forgiveness,
though we have rebelled against You. We have not
obeyed Your voice to walk in Your laws, which You
have set before us by Your servants the prophets. All
America/nation has transgressed Your law and
turned aside—we have not obeyed Your voice;
therefore, the curse is poured on us because we have
sinned against You. You have confirmed Your
words, which You spoke against us. All this evil has
come upon us, yet we did not make our prayer to
You, O Lord our God, that we might turn from our
iniquities and understand Your truth. Therefore,
You have kept watch over this evil and have brought
it on us, for You are righteous, O Lord, in all your
works, which You do, for we did not obey Your
voice. O Lord, according to all Your righteousness,
I beseech You, let Your anger and Your fury be
turned away from city name/nation because we have
become a reproach to all who are about us because
of our sins and because of the iniquities of our
ancestors. Now therefore, O God, hear the prayer
of Your servant and my supplications and cause
Your face to shine on us for Your sake. O my God,

incline Your ear and hear; open Your eyes and behold our desolation, for I do not present my supplications before You on the basis of our righteousness but on Your great mercy. O Lord, hear; O Lord, forgive; O Lord, listen and help; defer not for Your own sake, O my God, for Your people are called by Your name."

Chapter Ten

INTERCESSION: A LIFESTYLE

Wherefore he is able also to save them to the uttermost
that come unto God by him, seeing he ever liveth
to make intercession for them.
HEBREWS 7:25

Standing in the Gap

Intercession is truly a divine walk of love. Not only is it a walk of love, but it is a lifestyle to be lived out by all believers. Although not everyone may be called to be an intercessor—a watchman on the wall day and night— everyone who walks with God will be called on to pray intercessory prayers. If you have a lost loved one, hurting neighbor, or sick friend, your prayer of intercession is what will make the difference in that individual's life.

Intercession is standing in the gap between man and God for any given situation. It is moving the resources of the infinite on behalf of others. It is building a bridge or a highway between hell and heaven. It is freeing man from the spiritual forces of darkness that bind him and imploring God to be merciful and save him. It is hard work and requires a humble heart, willing to submit to the needs and burden of God.

How to Recognize a Burden

A burden is often recognized as a weight or depression on your spirit or heart, accompanied by a feeling of intense concern toward a person or about a situation. Every burden begins in the heart of God. God then looks for a vessel that will bear that burden. God still creates or manifests His thoughts through the spoken word. And because the church is now His body and mouthpiece, He speaks things into existence through individuals in the church. This is why it is so important to enter into His presence and to take on the burden of God when you pray.

There is a distinct difference between praying your will from the abundance of your own heart and praying the will of God. This is why it is important to make sure your heart is clean, your motives are pure before God, and you have unloaded the cares of this life. When you begin to intercede for a soul or situation, it very well could be that your prayers are going to determine the outcome of that soul or situation.

Three Main Actions of Intercessory Prayer

Receiving a Burden

First, you will receive a burden from God. A burden is

a concern from God. There are two primary purposes for a burden: The first is to come in front of Satan. God knows the plans of Satan and is looking for an intercessor who will stand in the gap to destroy his plans. The second is to bring about God's will in a person, place, or situation. In John 17 we read of the prayer that Jesus prayed to accomplish the will of God in His disciples' lives.

There are two types of burdens: The first type of burden is an *emergency burden*. The emergency burden is recognized by a depression or heaviness in your spirit and a strong desire to pray *immediately*. It is often accompanied with overwhelming compassion and mercy. An emergency burden can come at any time and anywhere. Have you ever driven down a street and all of a sudden began to cry? This is because God has a burden for someone or everyone on that street, and He needs you to pray. You can pray the will of God into existence right there in your car as you drive by.

The second type of burden is called a *long-term burden*. A long-term burden is a concern from God that you carry on your heart until it lifts from your spirit. For example, a person who is called to the mission field may pray for a country for years before actually becoming a missionary to that country.

You will know that you have prayed a burden through to completion when you experience a release (or relief) in your spirit. This is accompanied with the peace of God and oftentimes the joy of the Spirit. It is similar to the feeling that a mother and father experience after the birth of their child.

Spiritual Warfare

Spiritual warfare is the action of working a burden through. It is the act of engaging in a war or a conflict of any type for a religious or moral purpose.

In the Old Testament, warfare was a way of life, especially when taking over enemy territory. In the New Testament, we learn that our warfare is not against flesh and blood, but against spiritual principalities and powers. These powers are instrumental in blinding the minds of people and keeping them from receiving the gospel (II Corinthians 4:4). The apostle Paul referred to spiritual warfare in several epistles. (See II Corinthians 10:3-6; Ephesians 6:10-19; I Timothy 1:18-19; II Timothy 2:4.)

When you are engaged in spiritual warfare, you are rising up and taking authority over Satan and his schemes. You are directly addressing Satan and his kingdom. You are not fighting to see who is going to win; you are exercising your spiritual authority to put Satan in his rightful position, which is under the feet of Jesus Christ (Ephesians 1:17-23).

Those who have obeyed Acts 2:38 and hold fast to the doctrine of the oneness of God exercise spiritual authority from a position of being in Jesus Christ. Therefore the name of Jesus is working for you twenty-four hours a day. Jesus has all authority in heaven and earth (Matthew 28:18), and we access that authority and power when we invoke the name of Jesus! Jesus is the head of all principalities and powers, and all things have been placed under His feet. When you are in Christ, you are above all principalities and powers, and all things are under your feet.

Holiness and the Word are very important in spiritual warfare and are directly related to a person's level of authority in the spirit world. Why? Because Satan uses thoughts (words) to attack our weak areas when we begin to pray and make intercession. If our lives are not pure and full of the Word, he can capture our minds through thoughts contrary to Scripture, for example unworthiness, guilt, condemnation, vain glory, pride, selfishness, etc. He does this to refocus our burden and intercession for others back onto ourselves. Therefore, the purer our vessels are, the greater faith and authority we will exercise because we are not only waging war in faith, but we are also standing on the Word of God with a clear conscience. And when we know our vessel is pure and our position is in Jesus Christ, the enemy has no offense or defense. (See II Corinthians 10:3-6.) Holiness and the Word also release angelic assistance. (See Daniel 10:12; I Corinthians 11:10.)

Spiritual warfare is often characterized by speaking in tongues with an intensity and a directive to destroy satanic strongholds. (A stronghold is a pattern of thinking from which demonic powers rule.)

Isaiah 9:5 says, *"For every battle of the warrior is with confused noise, and garments rolled in blood."* Isaiah 10:27 says, *"And it shall come to pass in that day, that his burden shall be taken away from off thy shoulder, and his yoke from off thy neck, and the yoke shall be destroyed because of the anointing."*

Spiritual warfare is also characterized by speaking directly in a known tongue to the powers controlling a situation. This is how Jesus overcame Satan's temptations in the wilderness: *"Get thee hence, Satan: for it is written, Thou shalt worship the Lord thy God, and him only shalt thou serve"* (Matthew 4:10).

When exercising your authority to possess a place or overcome a situation for the will and glory of God, you may pray a prayer like this: "I take authority over every spirit of error. I bind every spirit of false doctrine, and I loose apostolic doctrine and the revelation of the knowledge and the power of the oneness of God." For it is written, *"They also that erred in spirit shall come to understanding, and they that murmured shall learn doctrine"* (Isaiah 29:24).

It is during warfare that you will exercise your mighty weapons by calling on the name of Jesus, pleading His blood, exercising the authority of His Spirit, standing in His righteousness, speaking His Word, understanding the victory of Calvary, knowing who God is, and putting on the whole armor of God.

You may ask: How do I know when I am involved in warfare? If you are praying, you will notice a change in the way you are praying (discussed in the above paragraphs). Otherwise, the Holy Ghost (especially the gift of discerning of spirits), your discernment, and your knowledge of the Word will cause you to recognize when something is not of God. I Corinthians 2:14 says, *"But the natural man receiveth not the things of the Spirit of God: for they are fool-*

ishness unto him: neither can he know them, because they are spiritually discerned." Hebrews 4:12 says, *"For the word of God is quick, and powerful, and sharper than any twoedged sword . . . and is a discerner of the thoughts and intents of the heart."* Hebrews 5:14 states, *"But strong meat belongeth to them that are of full age, even those who by reason of use have their senses exercised to discern both good and evil."*

There are other signs of spiritual warfare. You may experience feelings of oppression (heaviness on your spirit), as in Acts 10:38: *"Jesus . . . who went about doing good, and healing all that were oppressed of the devil; for God was with him."* You may also recognize negative or perverse thoughts trying to come against your mind and trying to enter into your heart. In addition, you may experience physical illness, such as stomach cramping, nausea, headaches, and sinus problems. You may also experience a temporary loss of your thoughts. When you experience these signs of spiritual warfare it is of the utmost importance that upon recognition you immediately rebuke these symptoms. Speak directly to the spirit (if you know what it is) and/or symptom and command it to leave in the name of Jesus. Oftentimes, a sudden unexpected onset of stomach cramping, sinus problem, or nausea denotes a spiritual attack of either witchcraft or error. Take authority over these spirits, and you will experience almost, if not immediate, relief if indeed they are the cause.

It is important not to focus on spiritual warfare but to keep your eyes on Jesus. He will prepare you, and He will fight through you and for you. You want to focus on the kingdom of our Lord and Savior Jesus Christ, for they that are with us are more than they that are with them.

Travail

Travail is the action of birthing a burden. Once you have destroyed the enemies' stronghold, it is time to birth the will of God into existence. This was exemplified in Elijah's ministry. After he destroyed the prophets of Baal, he went on top of Mount Carmel and began to pray for rain. He knelt down and put his face between his legs, which was a position of giving birth at that time. The result was rain! Just like Elijah, you too can bring forth the rain of God's Spirit through travail.

Travail is a cry before God, and it is addressed to God. Where spiritual warfare is entered into to overcome Satan and his kingdom, travail is entered into to manifest God and His kingdom. It is often characterized by deep, intense weeping, groaning, and pleading. It comes from the innermost part of your being.

Travail can also be described as the prayer of compassion. It is holy and personal. It is associated with a very deep level of identification for the situation about which you are praying.

Intercessory prayer, and especially travail, is very taxing on the body and should be balanced. Praise and worship need to accompany intercessory prayer to restore strength.

*Although everyone is not called to be
an intercessor, everyone should know how
to pray an intercessory prayer.*

Chapter Eleven

CONCLUSION

Could it be that many religions of the world are experiencing growth because they give themselves to prayer? The followers of Islam pray five times a day. Satan perverts the principle of prayer and uses it for his glory. We have at our disposal all the resources we need to destroy the works of darkness and to live a victorious life in Jesus Christ. All we have to do is seek first the kingdom of God and His righteousness and all these things shall be added to us. It is time to pray, pray, pray, and pray some more!

The following poem was written by a great intercessor and dear friend of mine, Julie Ann Reynolds. It truly expresses the heart of one who spends time in the presence of the Holy One: Jesus!

Thank You, Lord, for desiring to meet with me,
Even to stoop to my station, to speak, to listen, to
    love,
Thank You—Thank You!

I love You with a heart that overflows with gratitude,
For I know my failures,
But You overlook them all to be with me.

How awesome—how amazing—
Your mercy, beyond words—beyond describing,
The desire of an immaculate God to meet with
A sinner like me.

Enfold Your desires around my heart,
So they will become my own,
I owe You all—I care about You, too,
How could I not, my friend—my friend
Thank You for meeting with me once again.

And somehow, in Your presence we become one,
And out of that union souls shall be born!

ABOUT THE AUTHOR

Kim Johnson was born and raised in a suburb of Chicago, Illinois. Her prayer life began as a child when she was taught by her grandmother to pray the "Our Father" prayer. Little did she know that her prayers and love for God, from a young age, would eventually lead her to an Acts 2:38 experience of being born again of water and Spirit. Just prior to Kim's conversion, she stepped down from her position as president of a graphic arts corporation. Even at that time, God was dealing with her about issues pertaining to righteousness and holiness. After leaving her career in graphic arts, she spent most of her time in intercessory prayer, teaching Bible studies, and assisting her local congregation. During the past 17 years of serving God, her ministry of prayer has been undergirded by the advice of elders who have given their lives to prayer. Today, Kim continues to give herself to the ministry of intercessory prayer. She possesses the necessary Biblical knowledge and experience to assist the prayer life of believers and non-believers alike. She continues to travel internationally teaching seminars on prayer.